This Coloring Book Belongs to :

_____

_____

I0480871

Thank you for choosing our book

Our aim is to provide the best boook companion for all our customers.

Our greatest satisfaction is to have created the suitable coloring book with the utmost attention to details, clear and sharp printing, high-quality papers and the perfect size.

If You Enjoy it , Please consider Leaving a review in <u>Amazon</u>

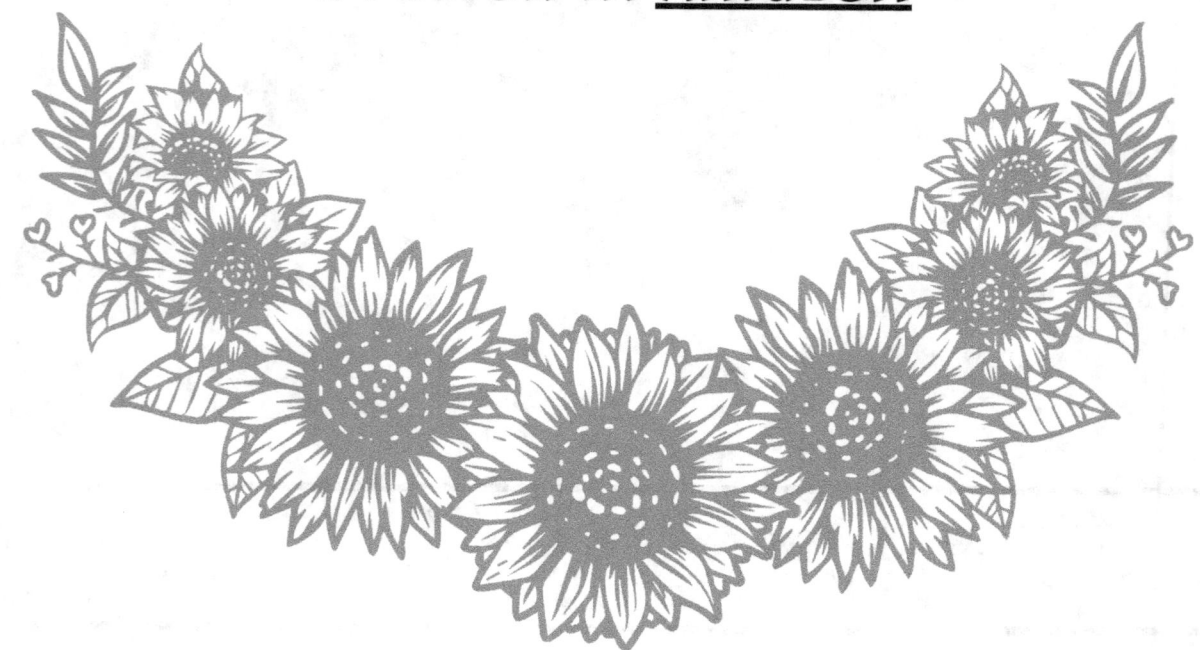

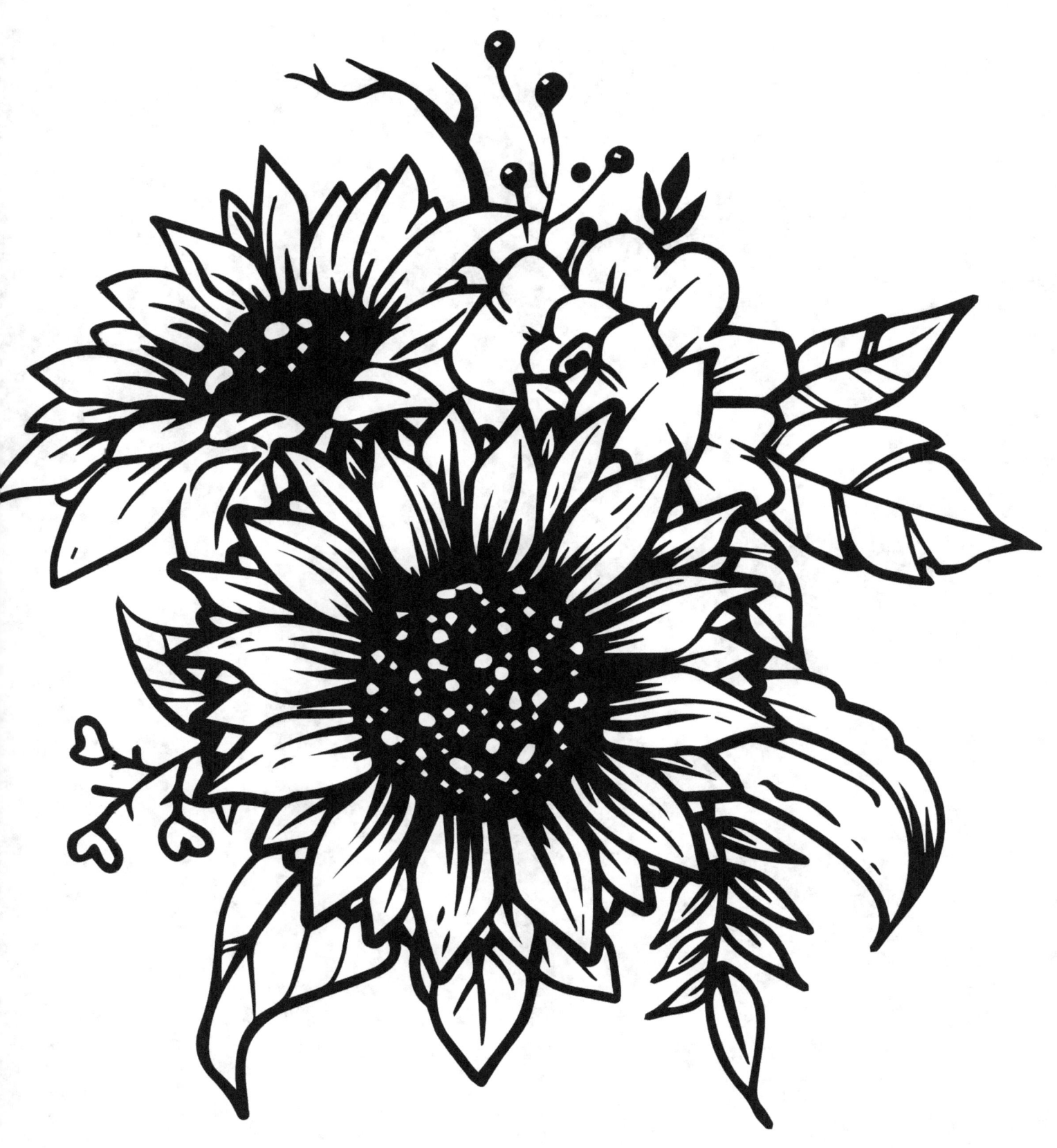

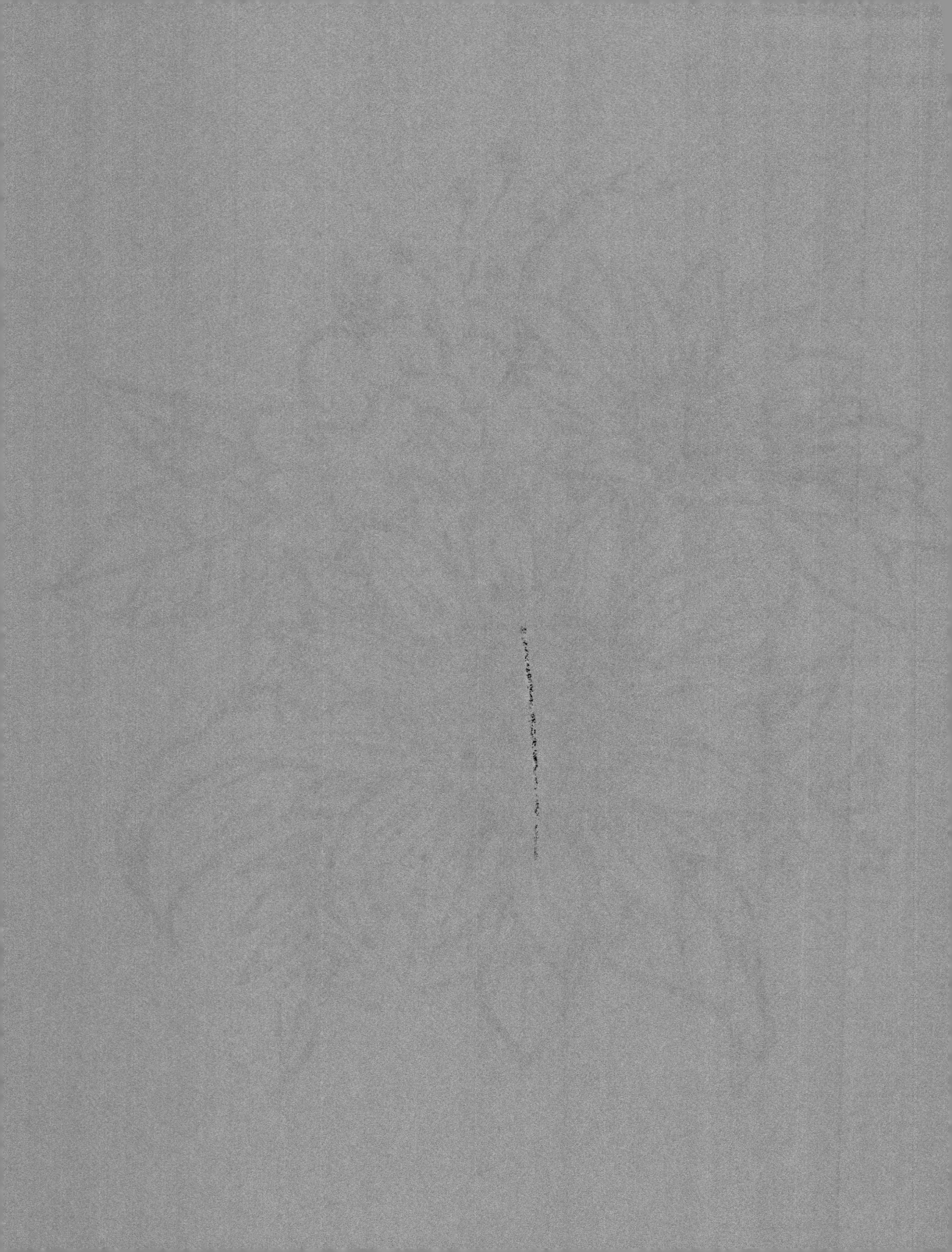

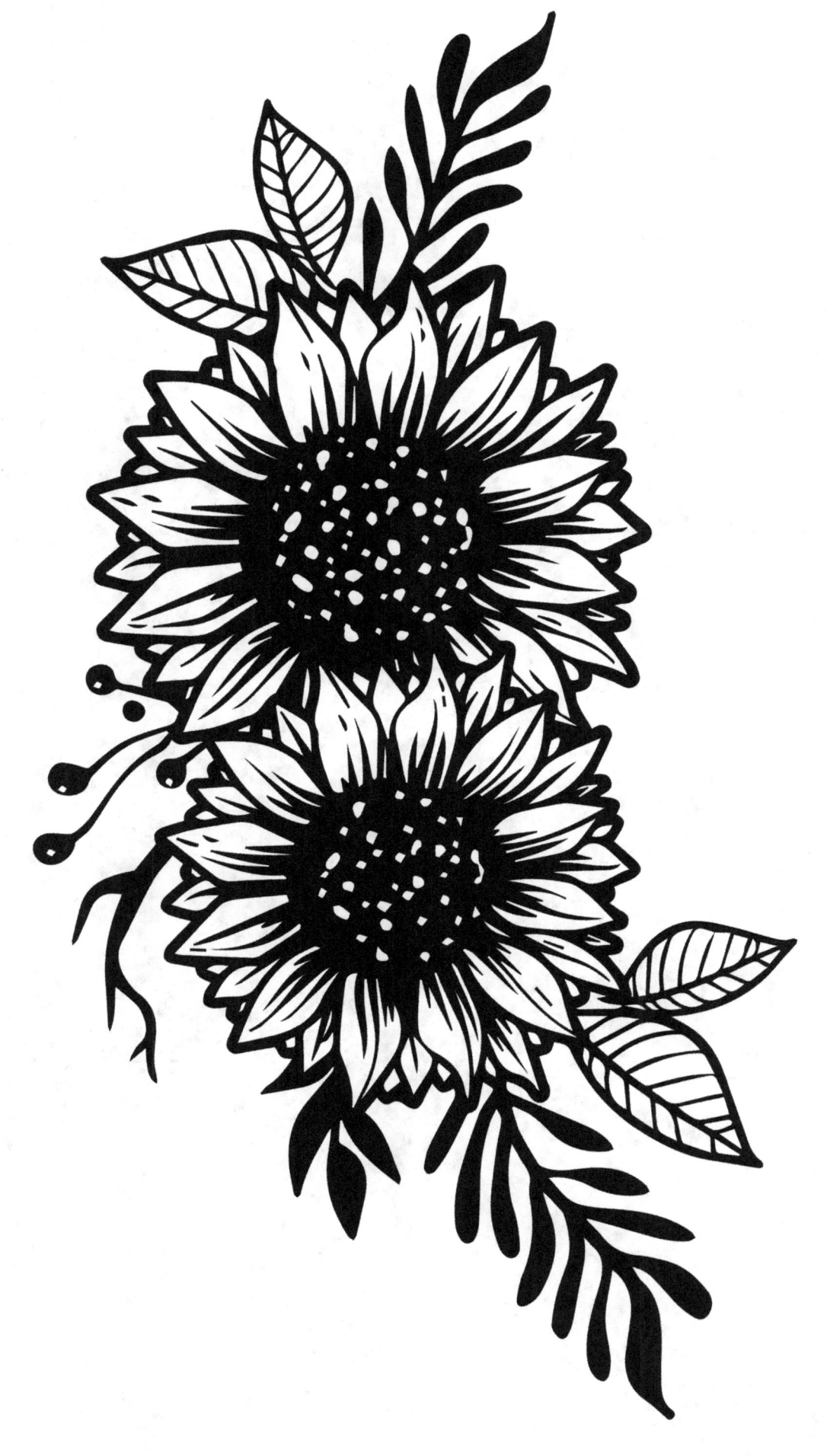

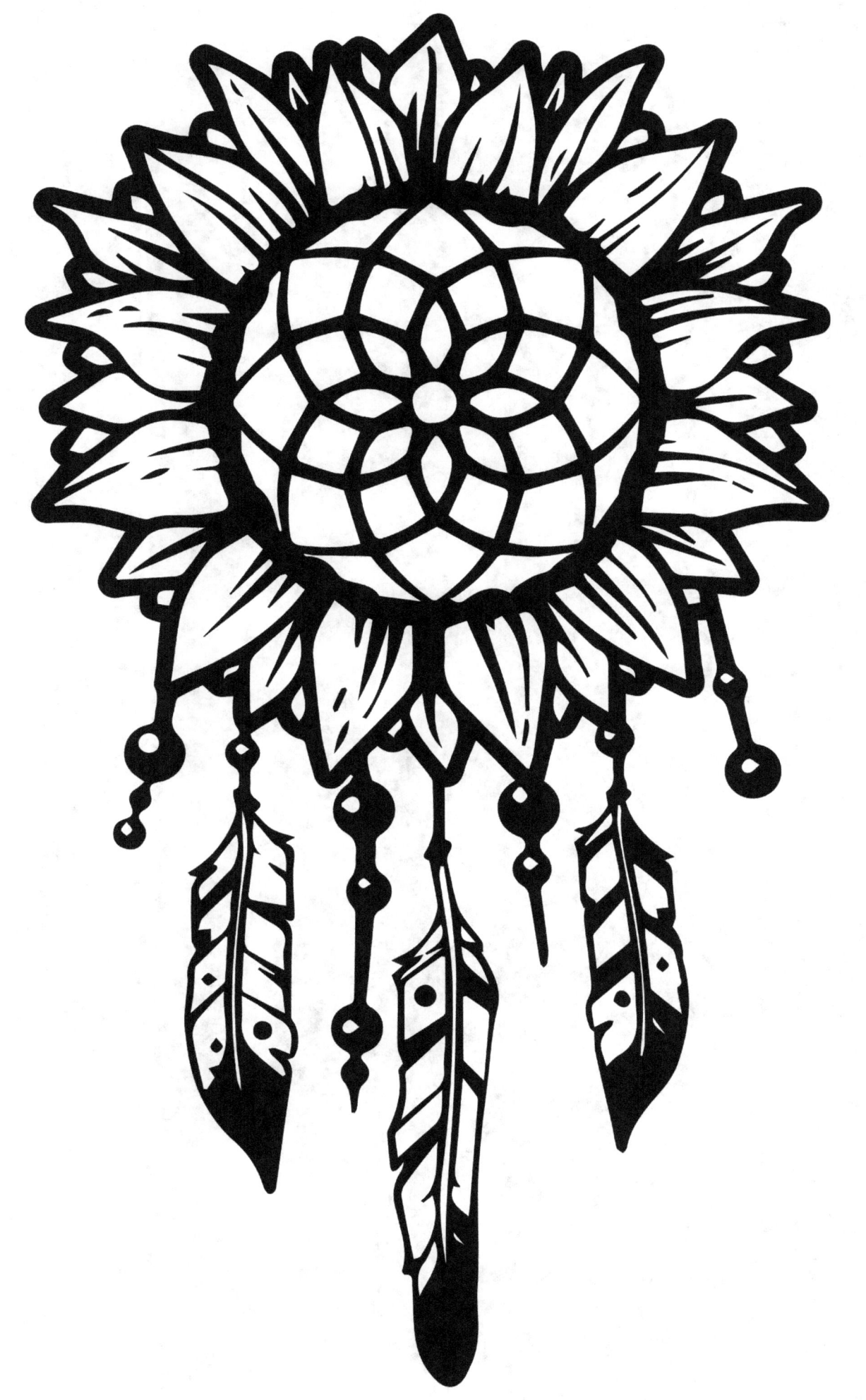

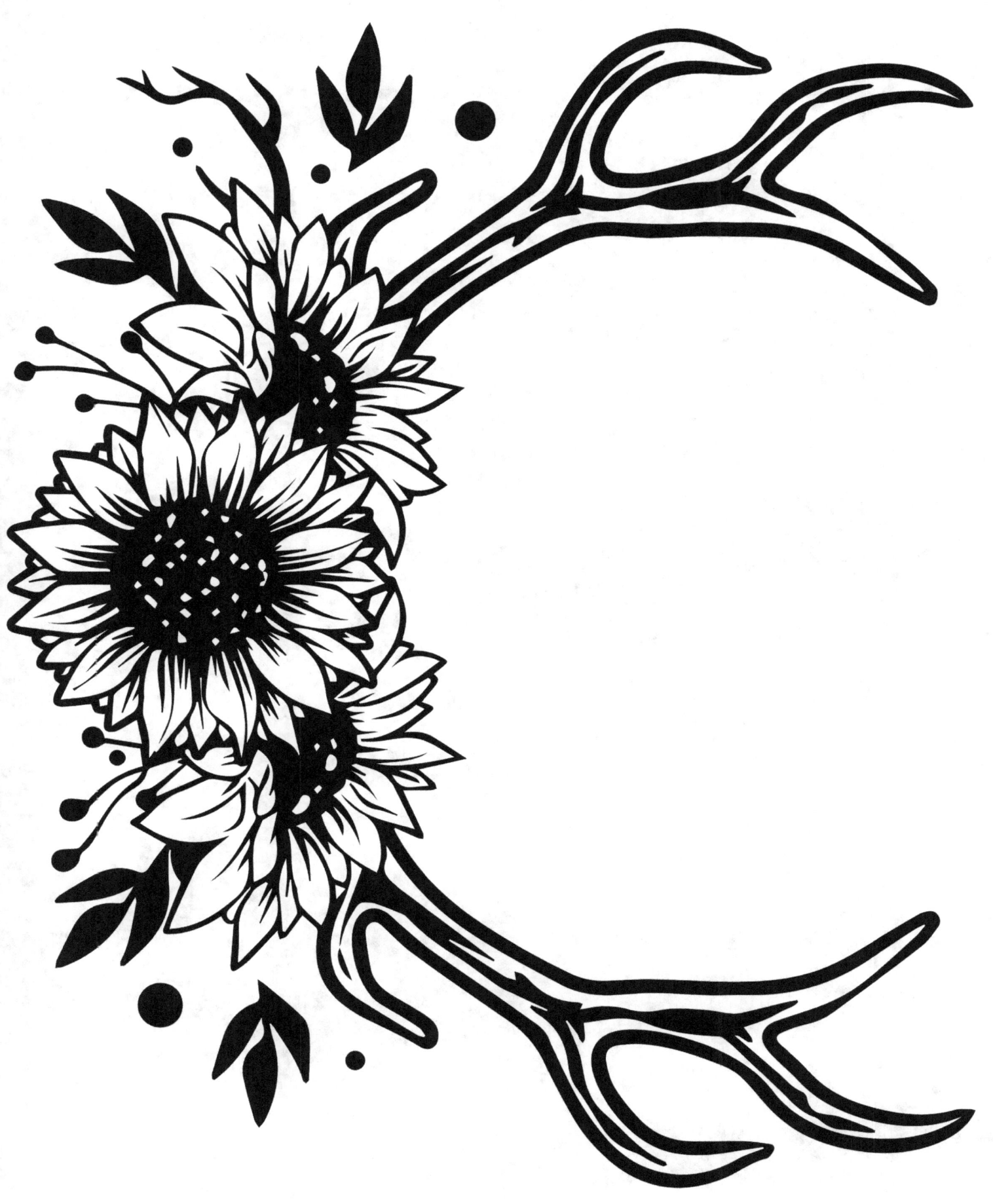

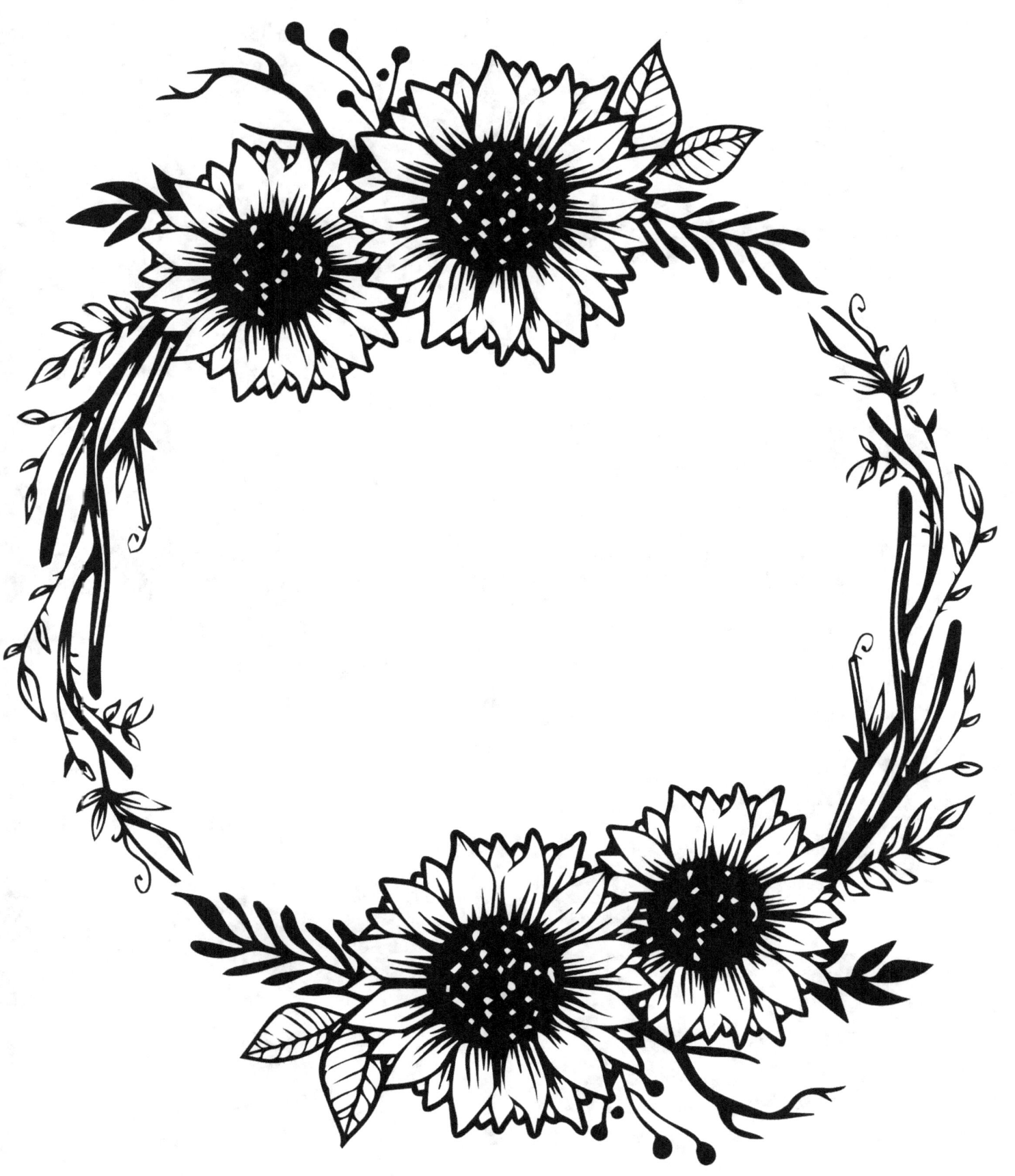

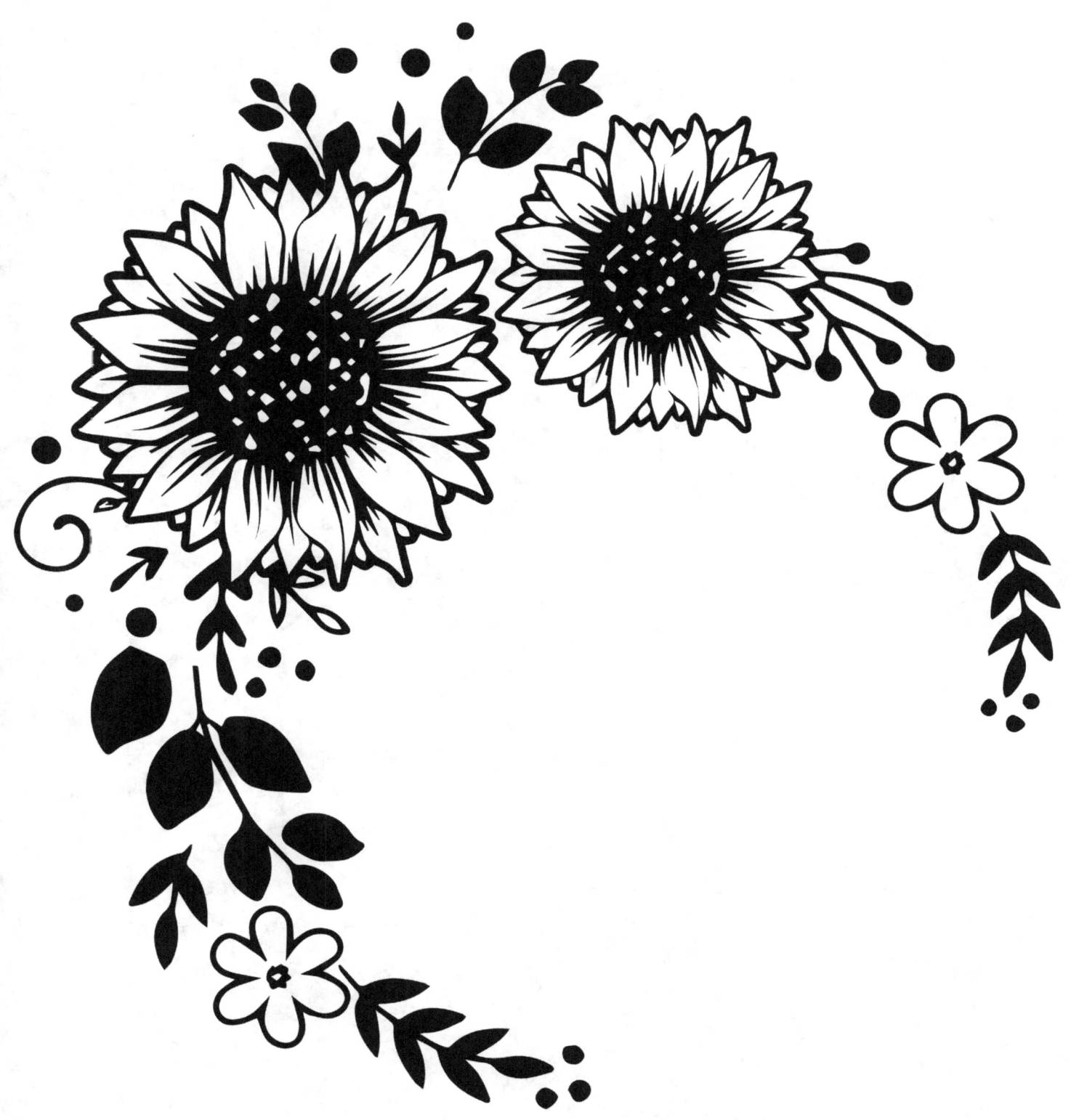

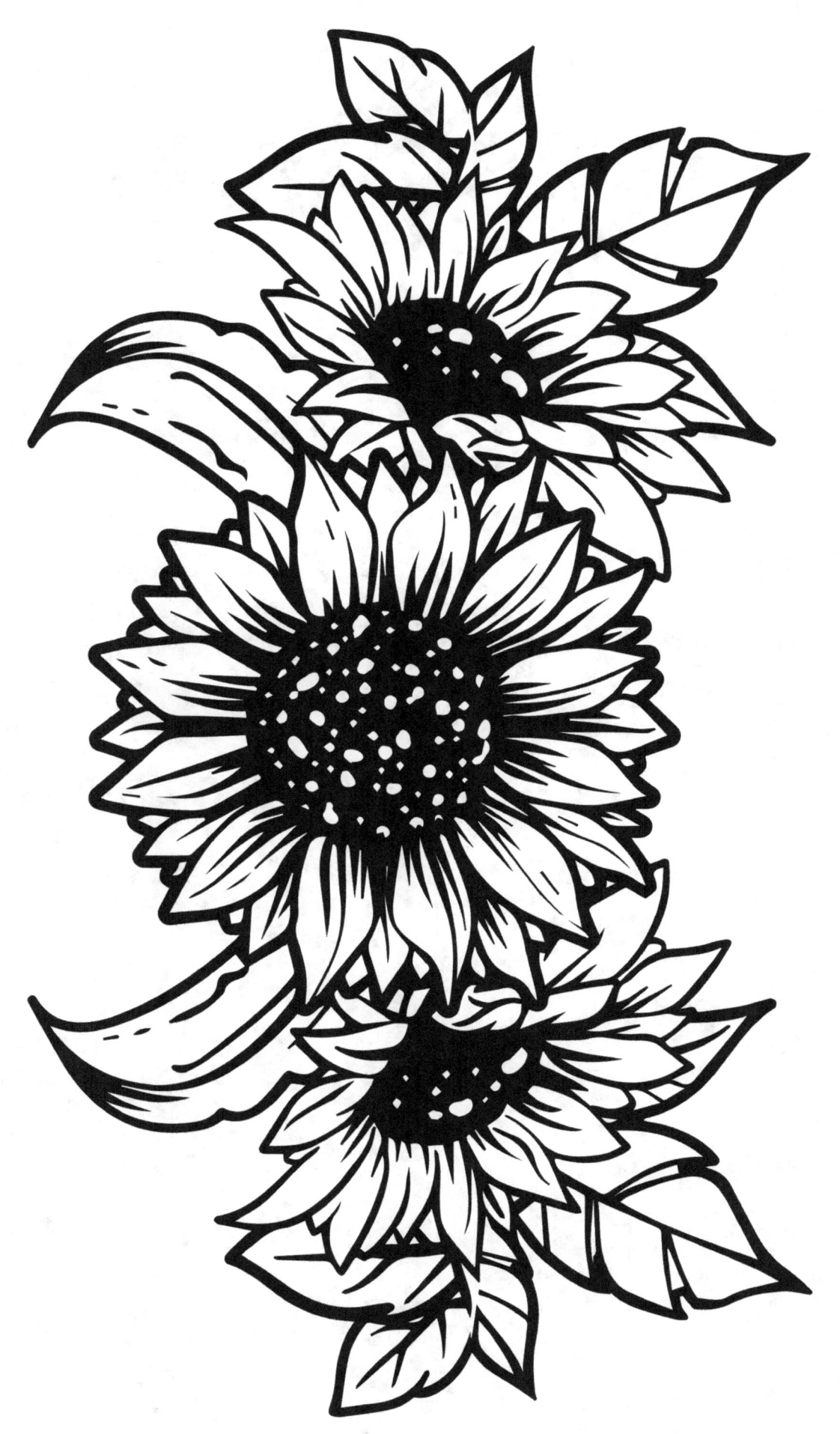

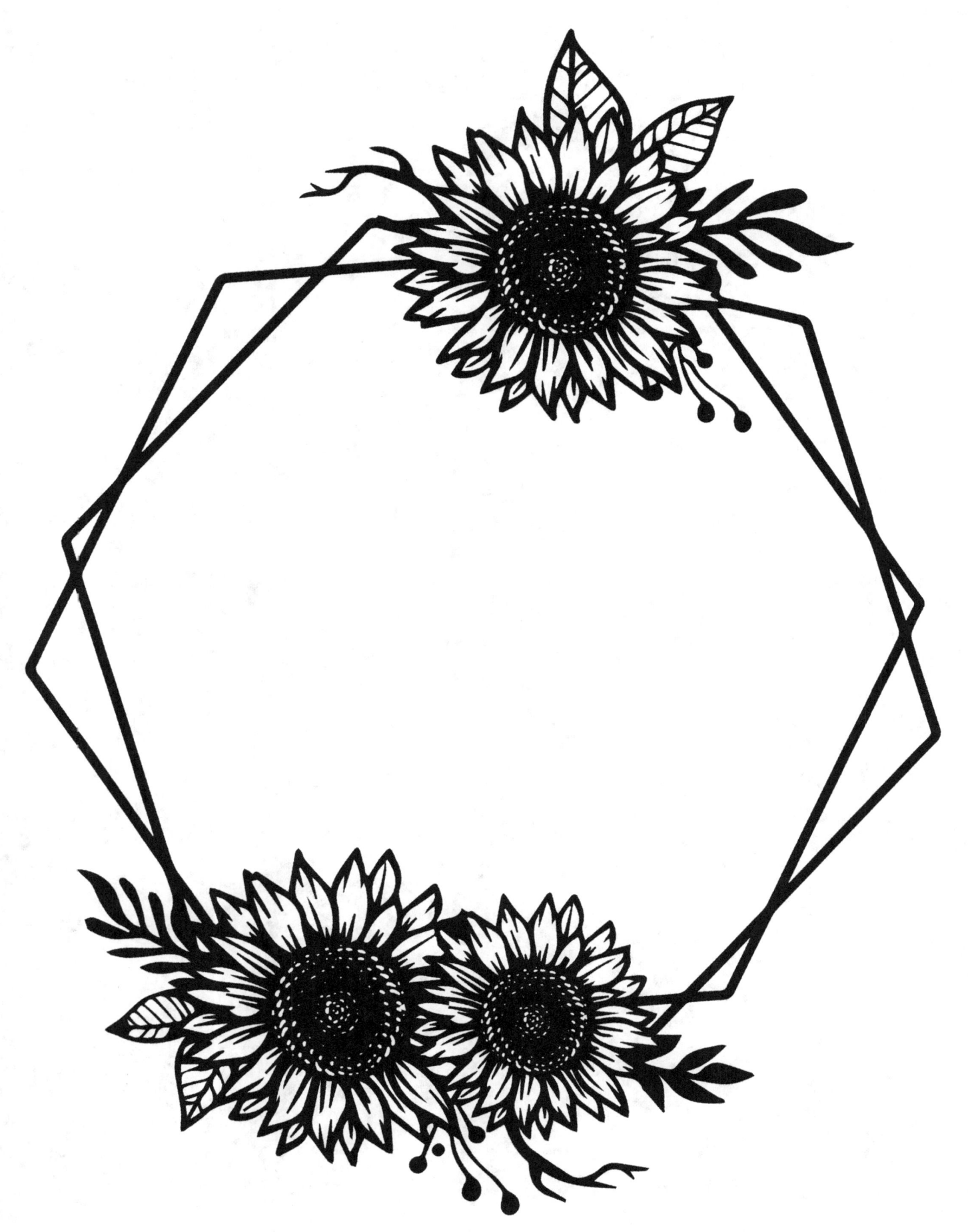

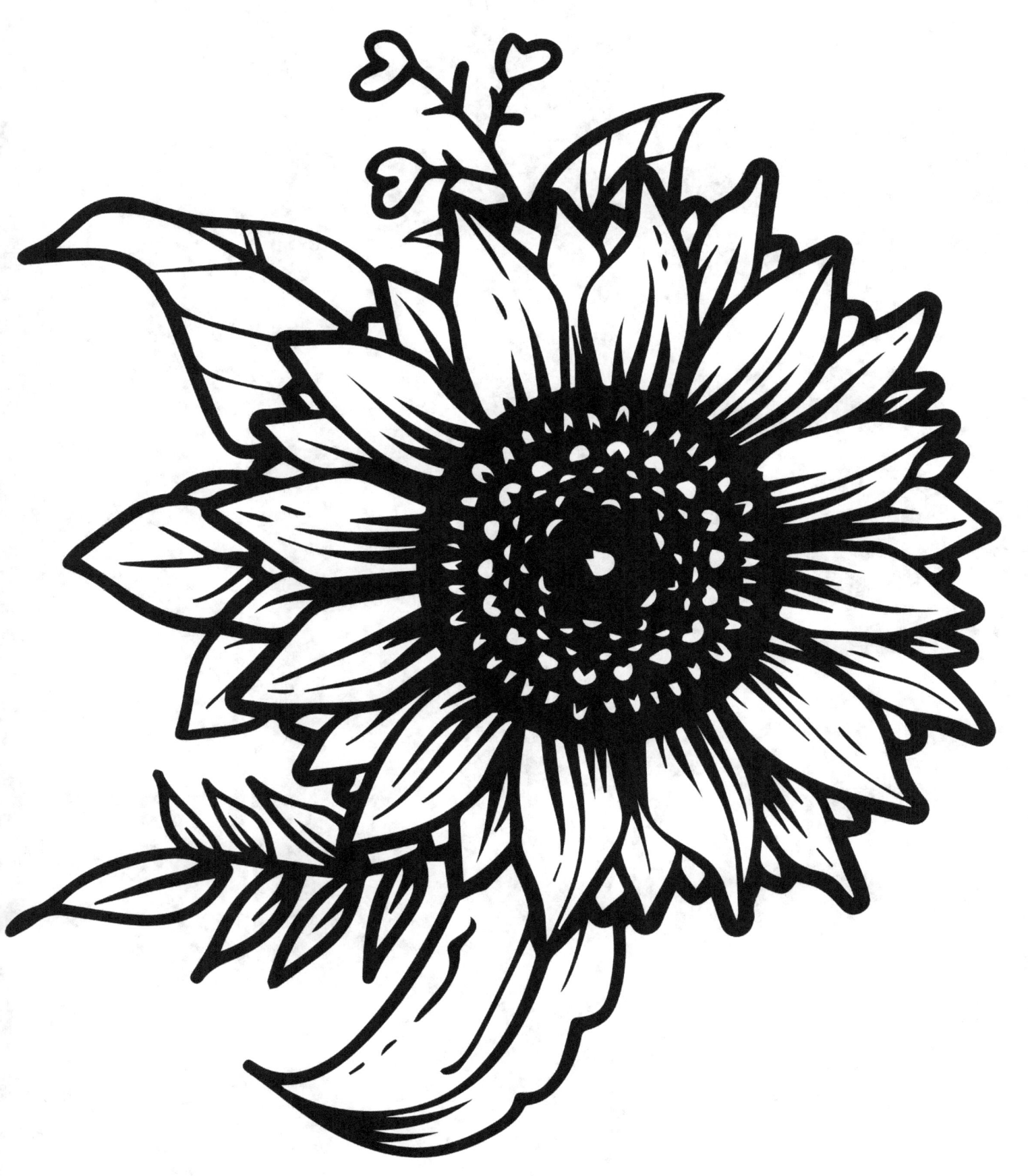

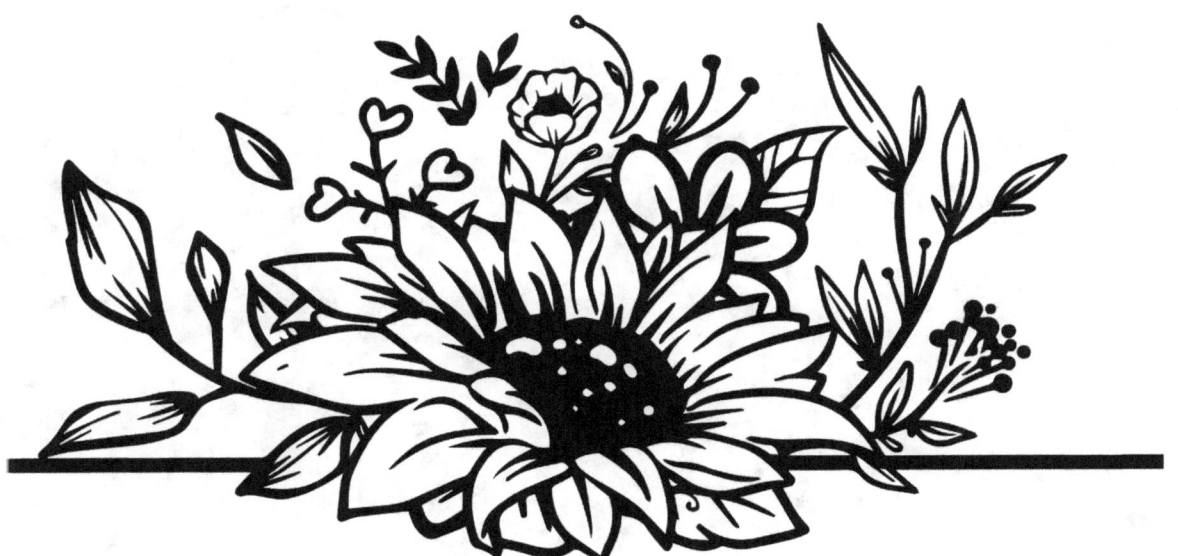

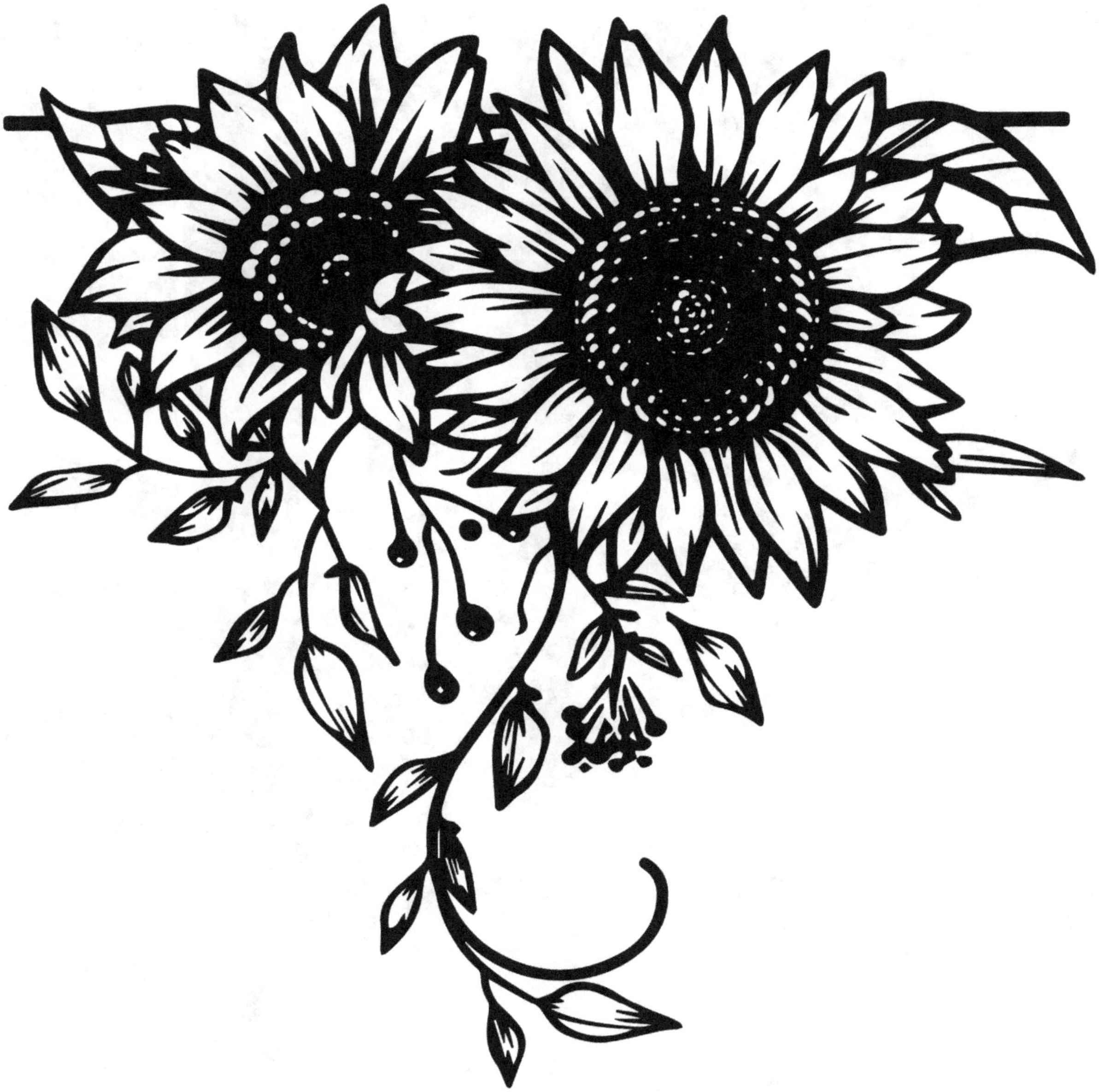

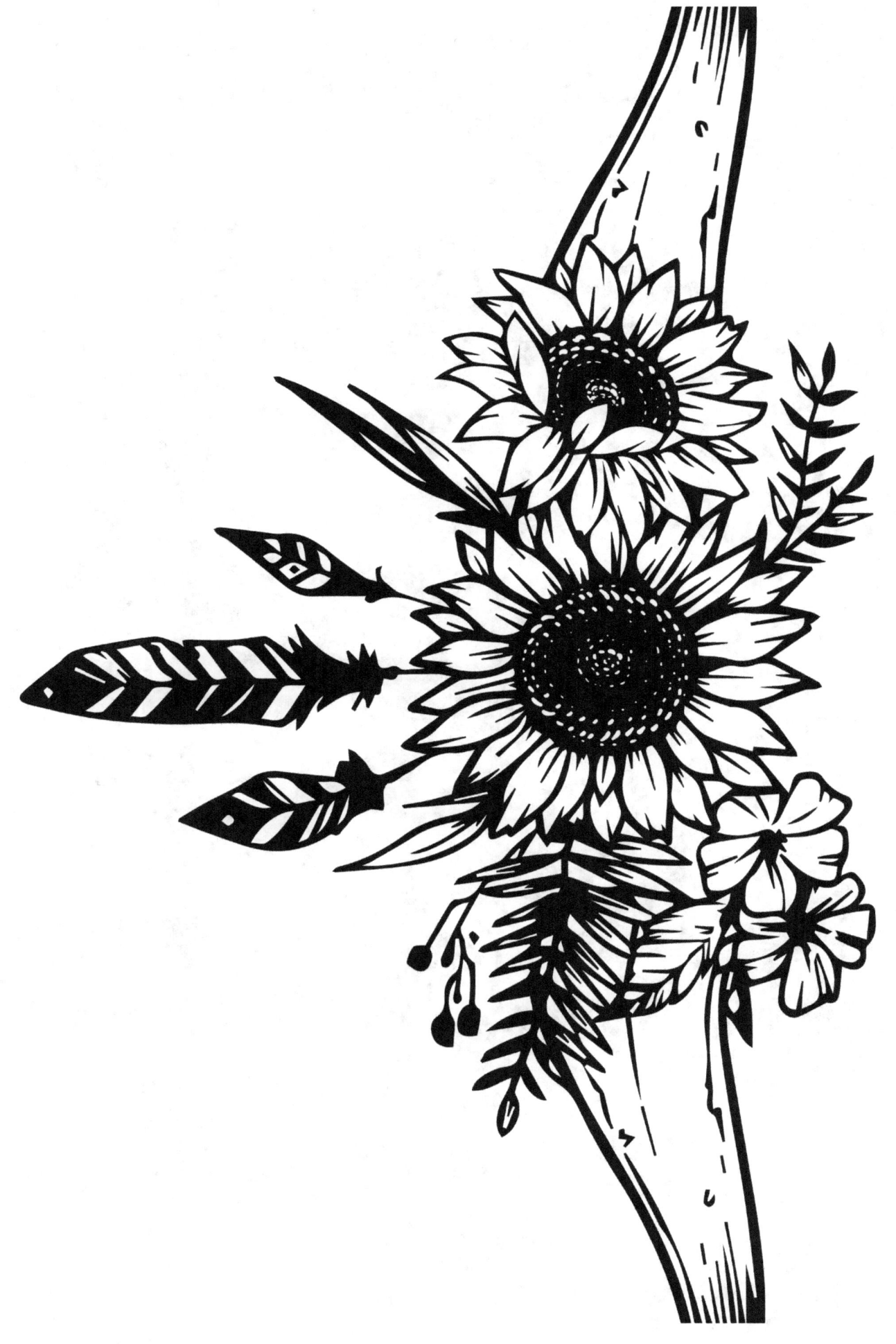

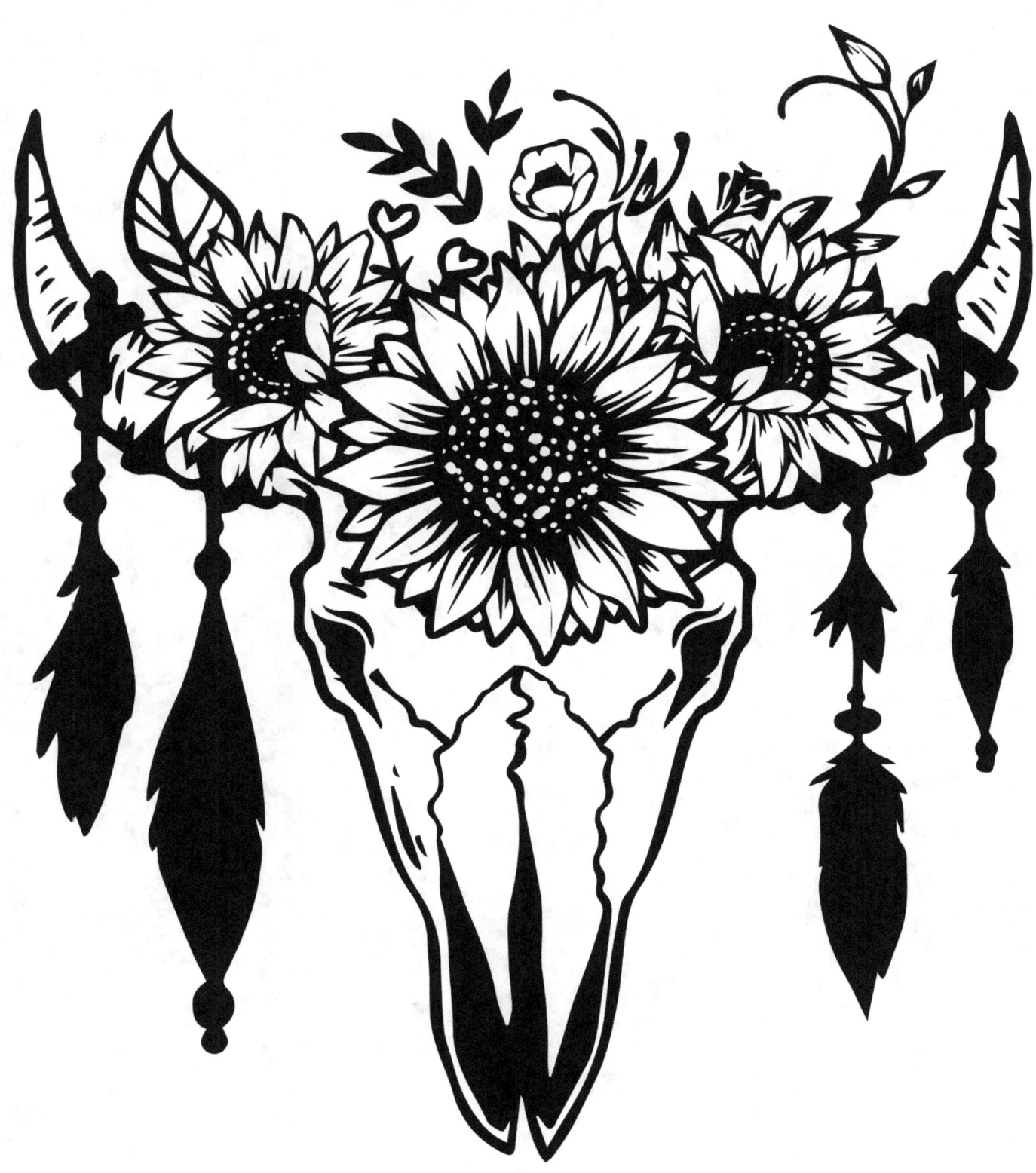

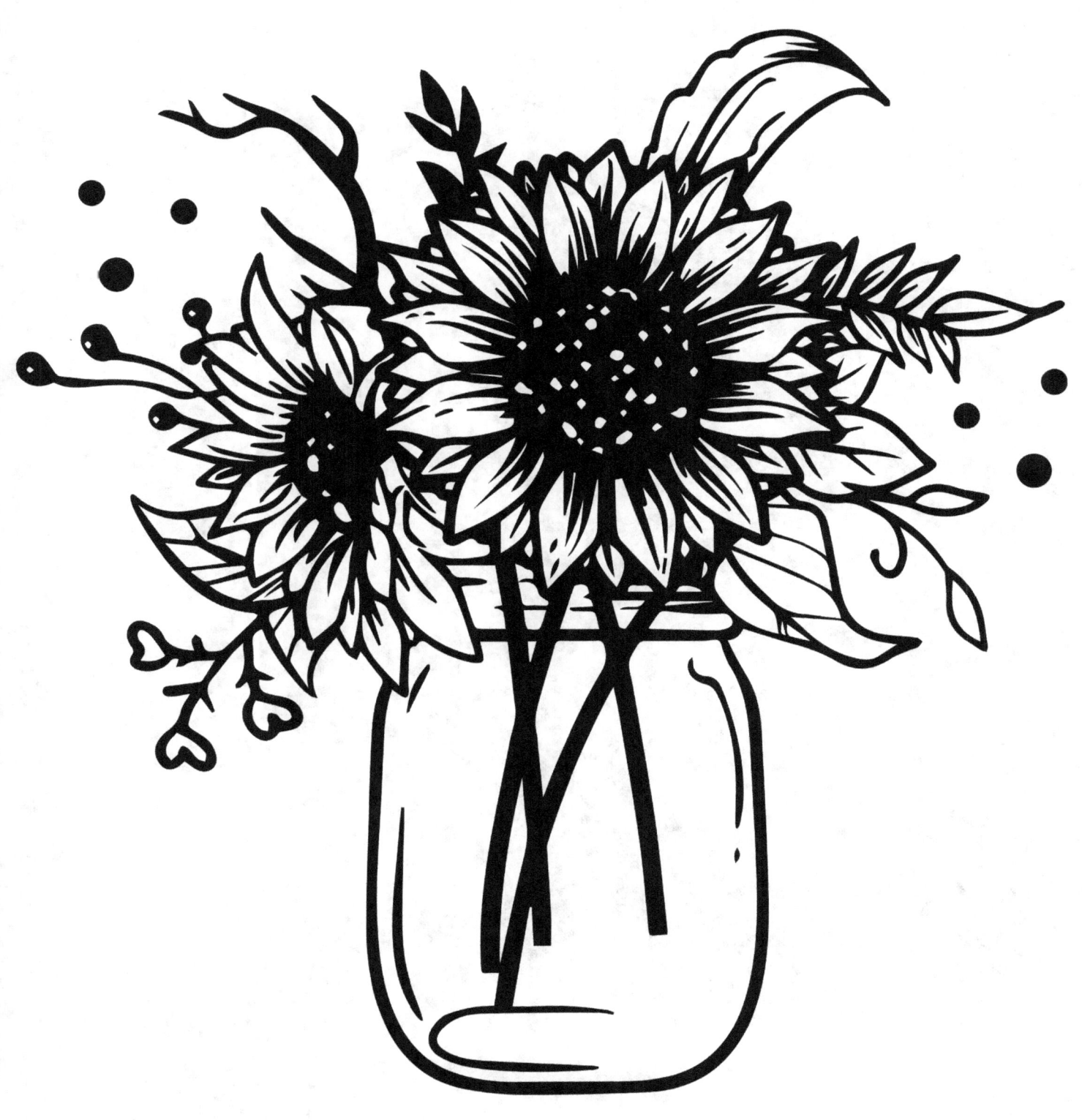

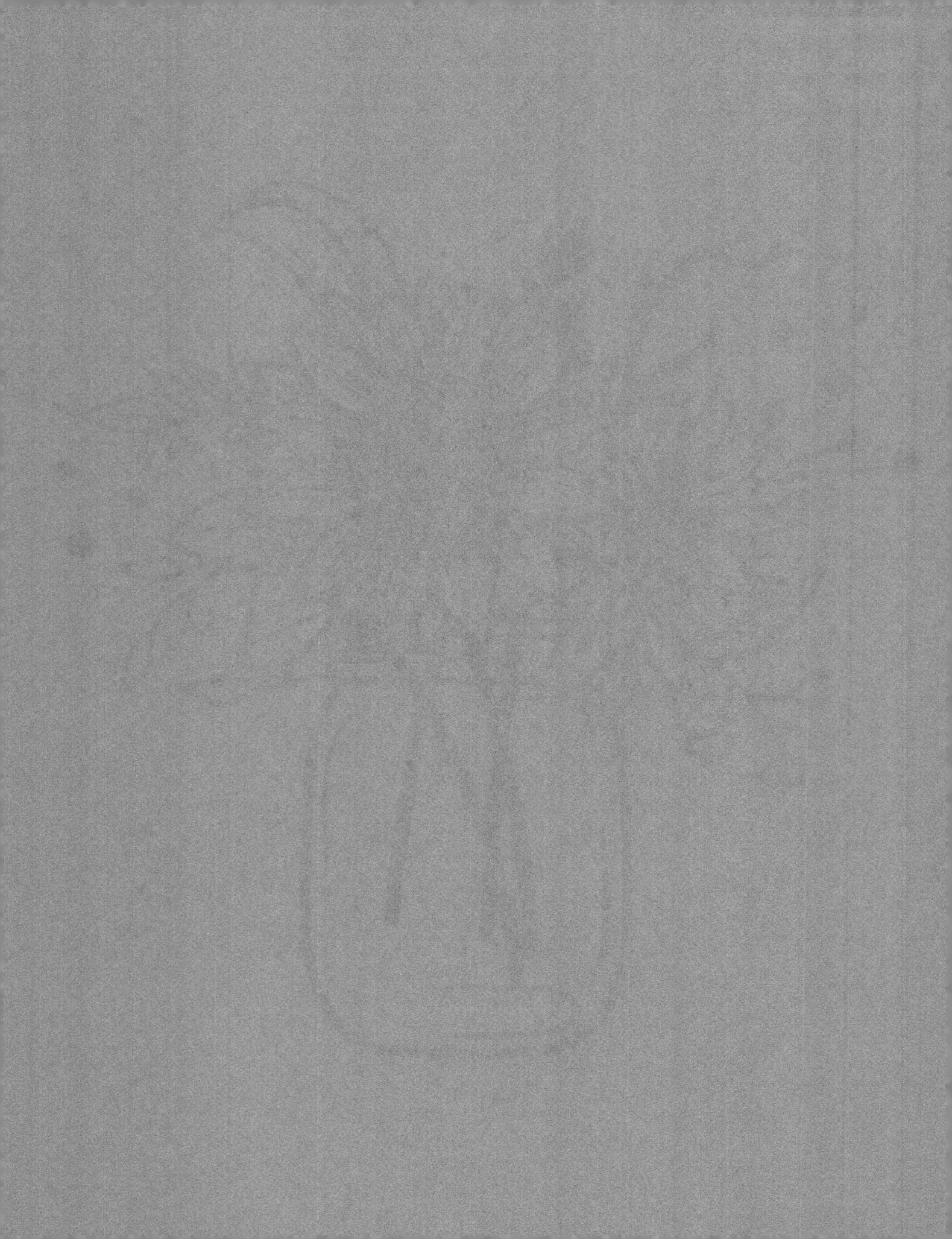

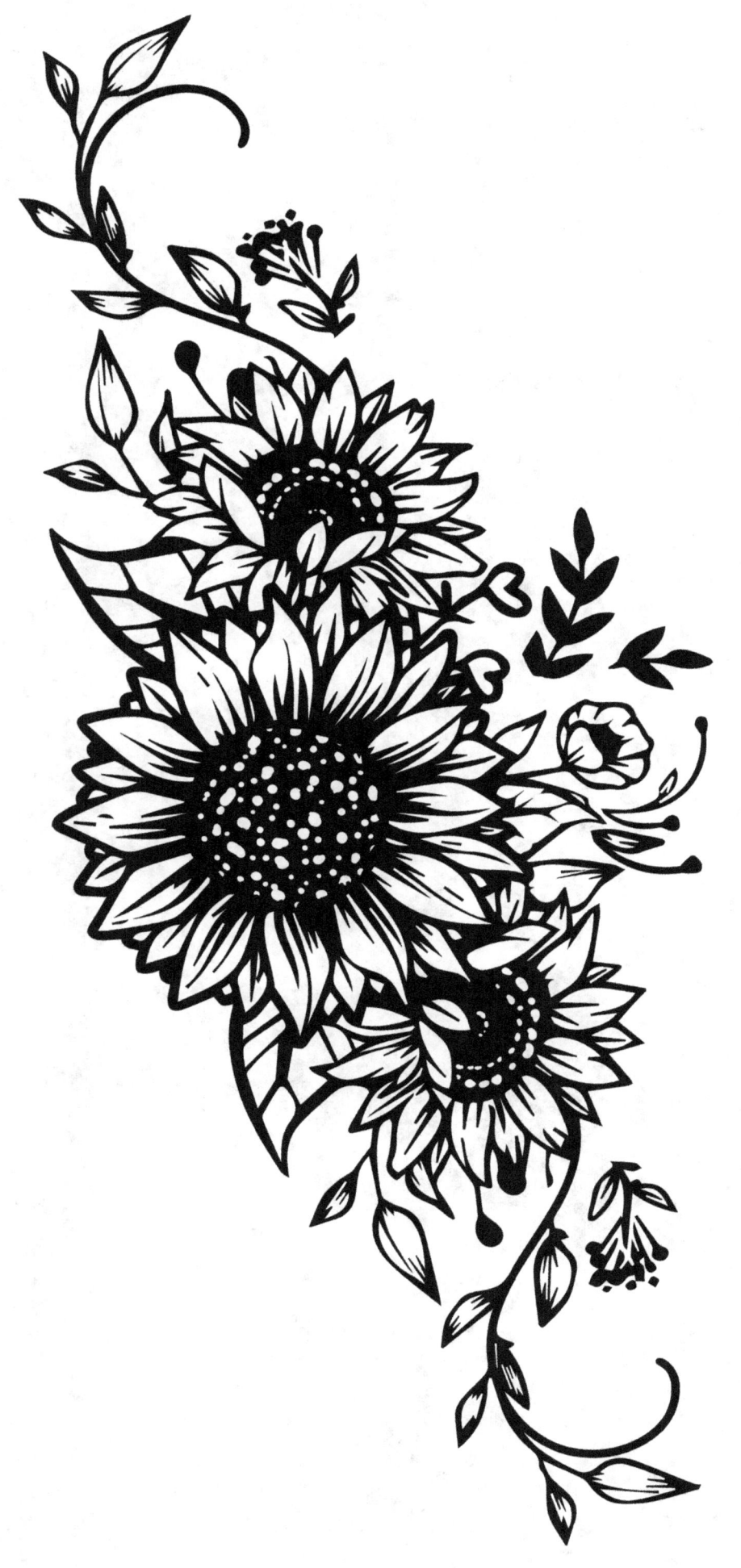

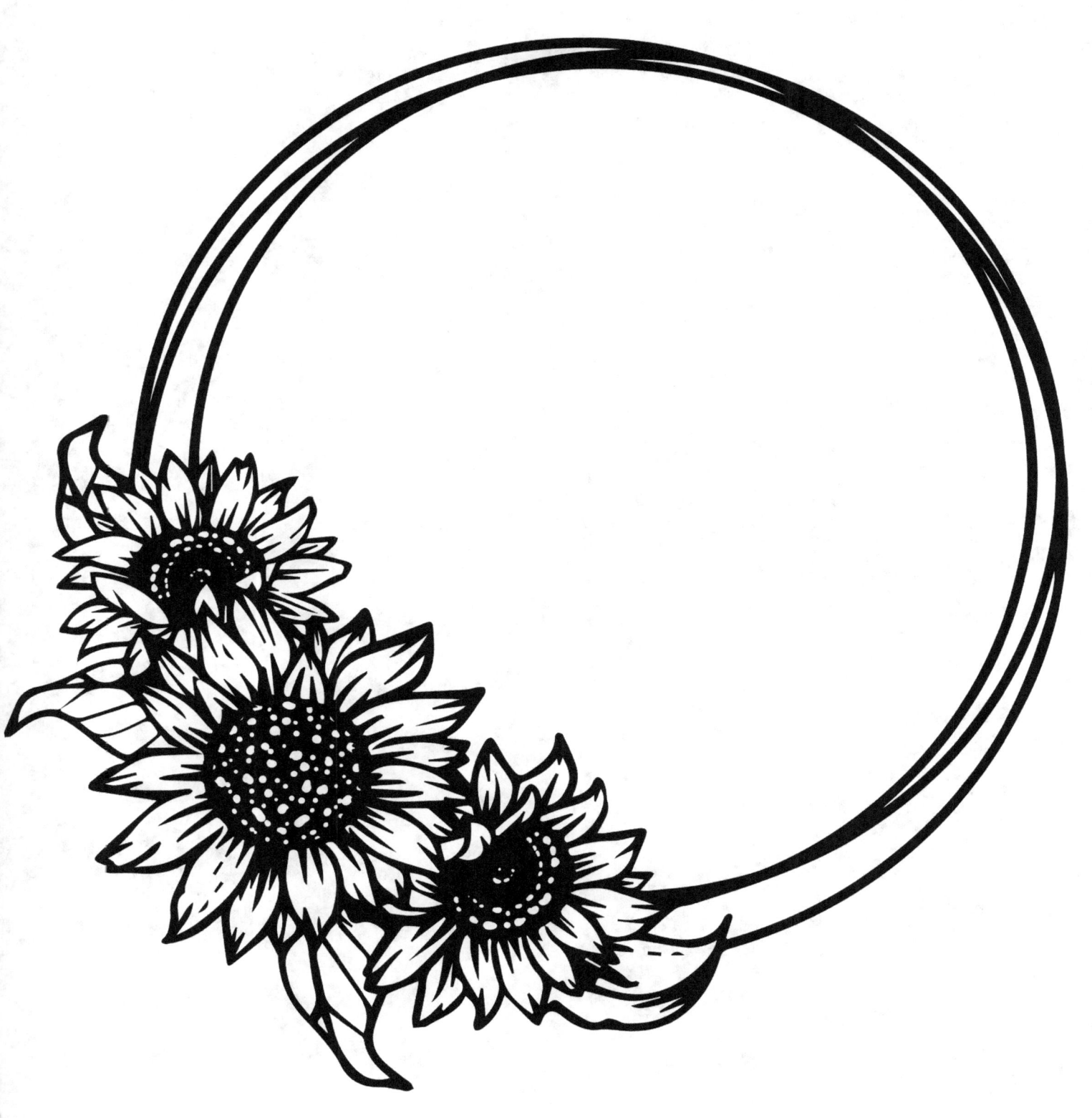

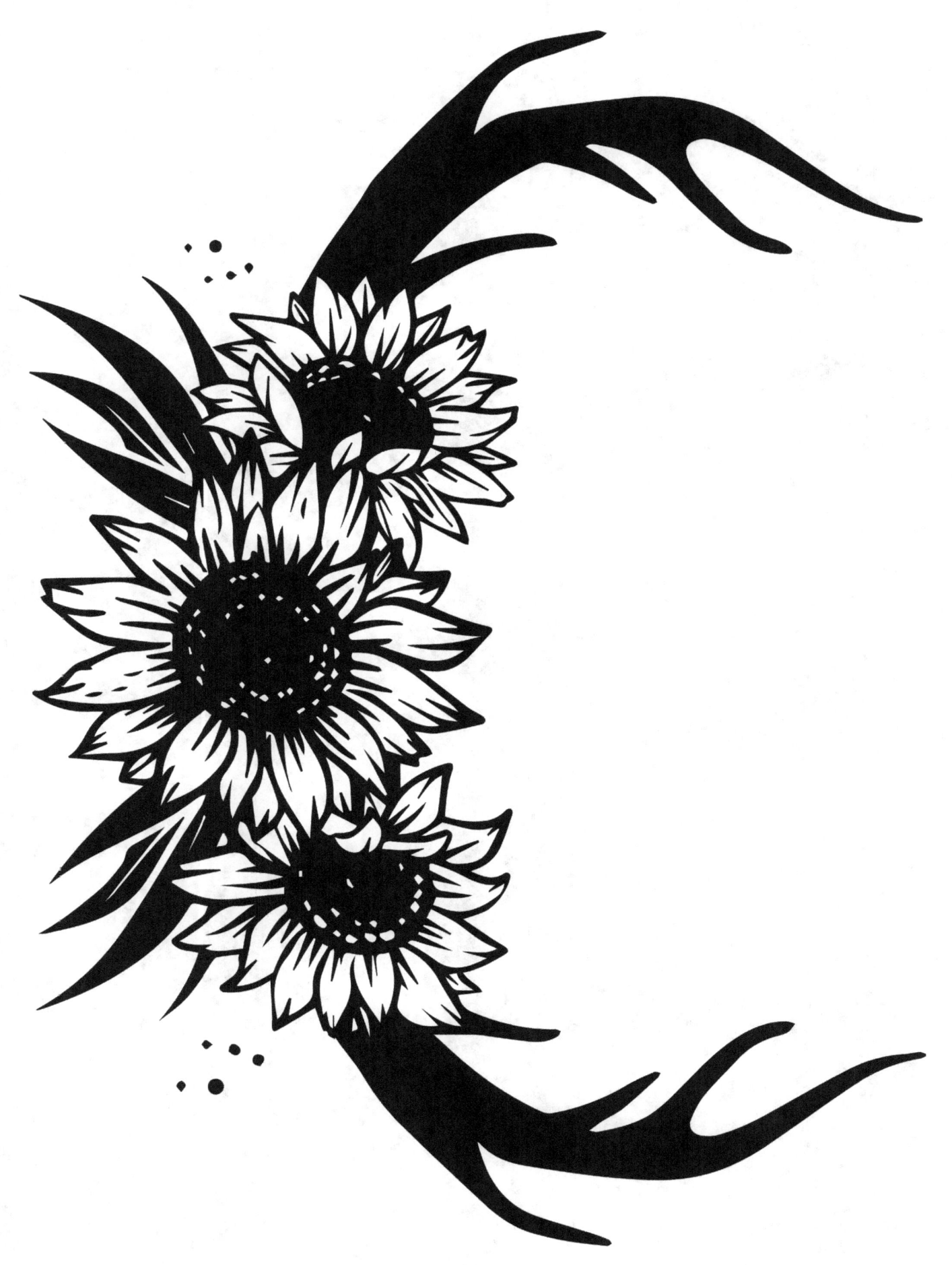

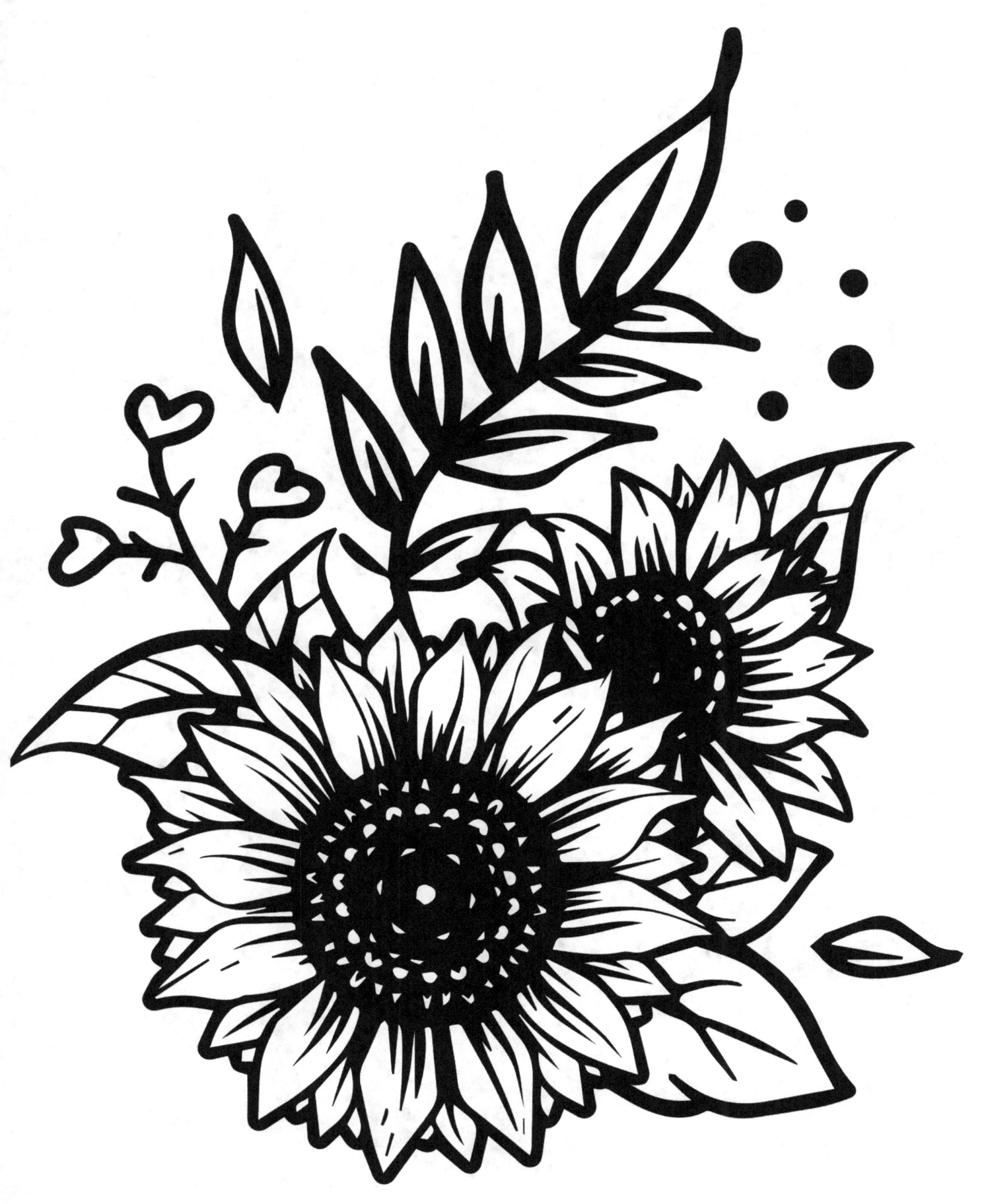

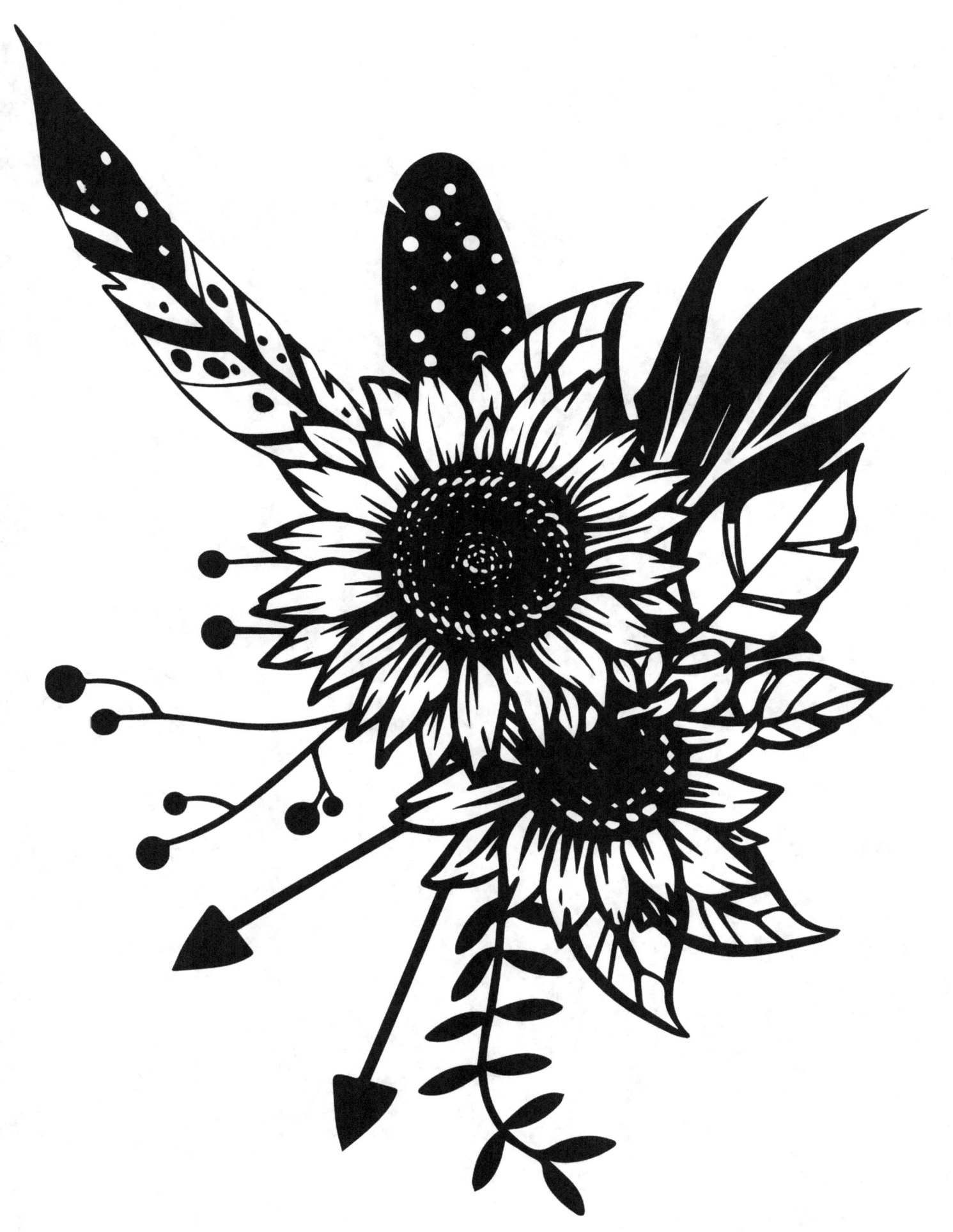

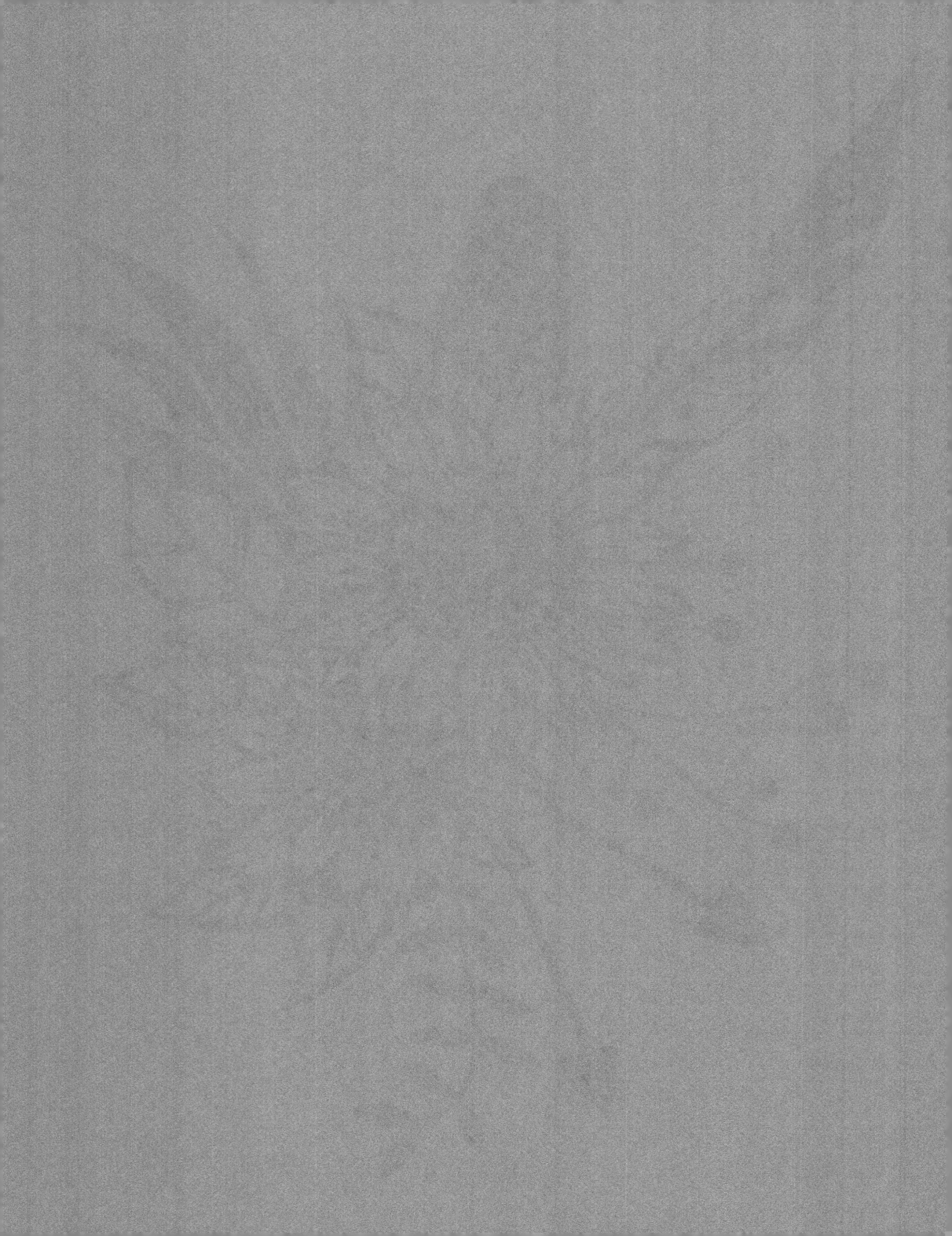

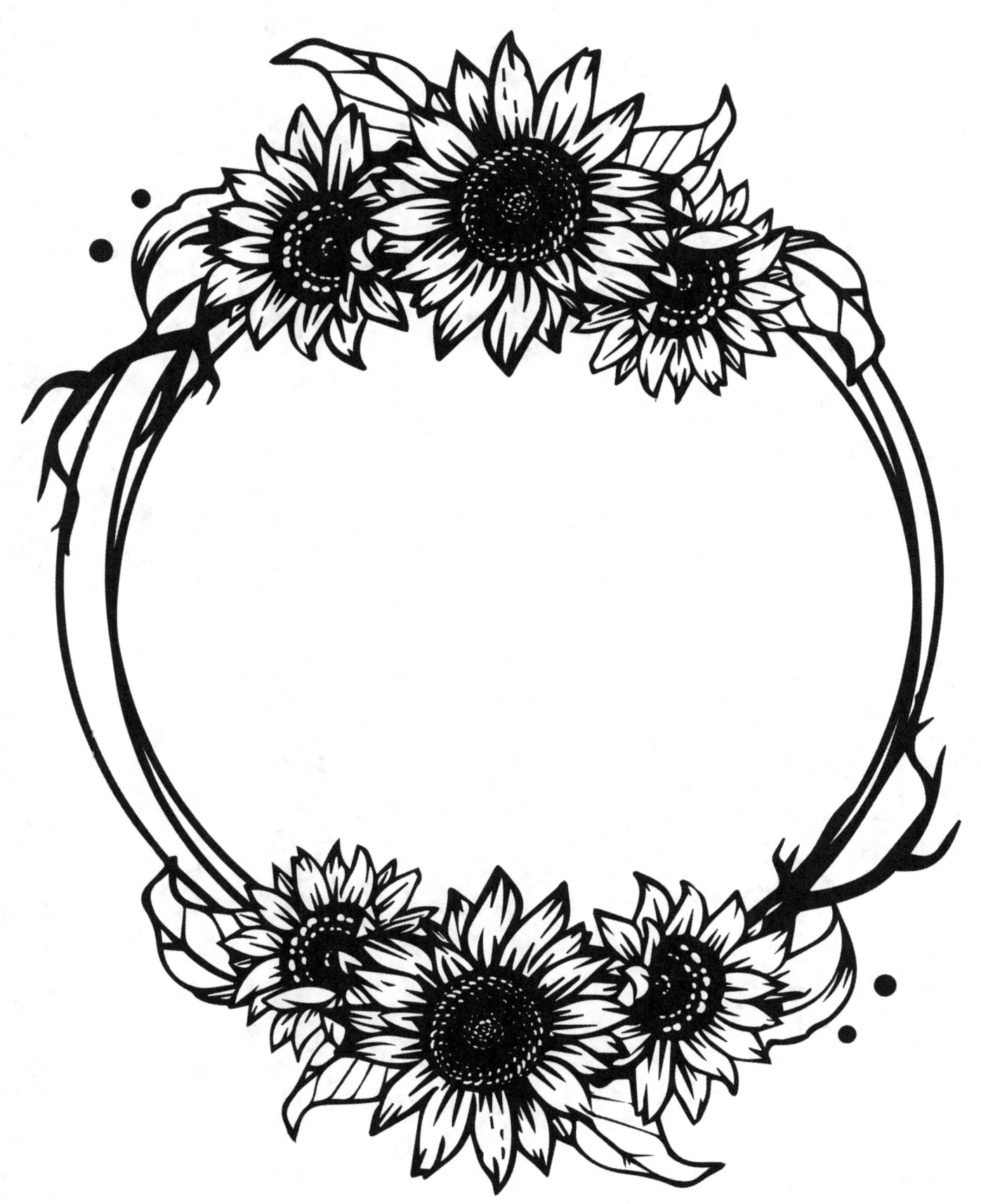

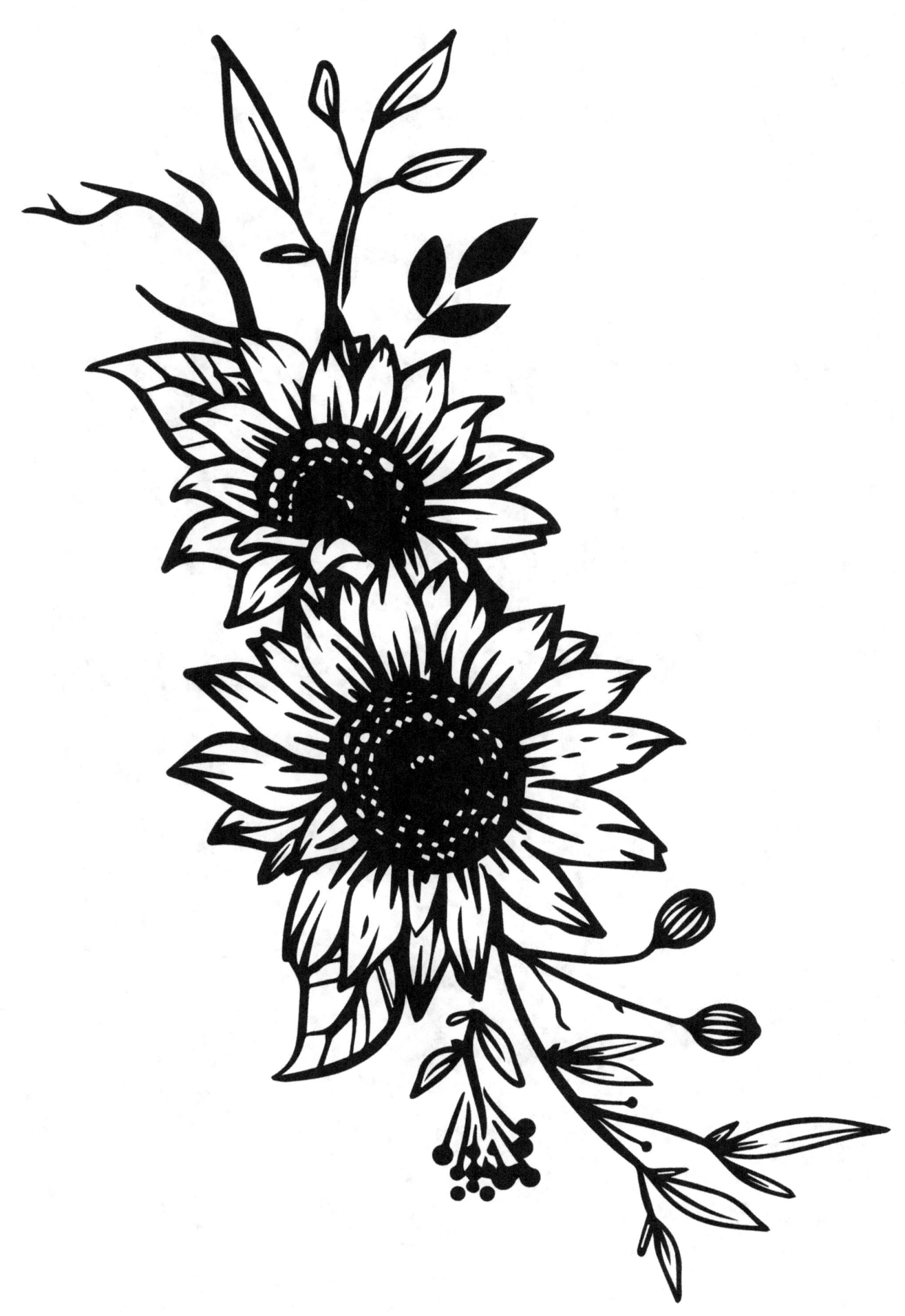

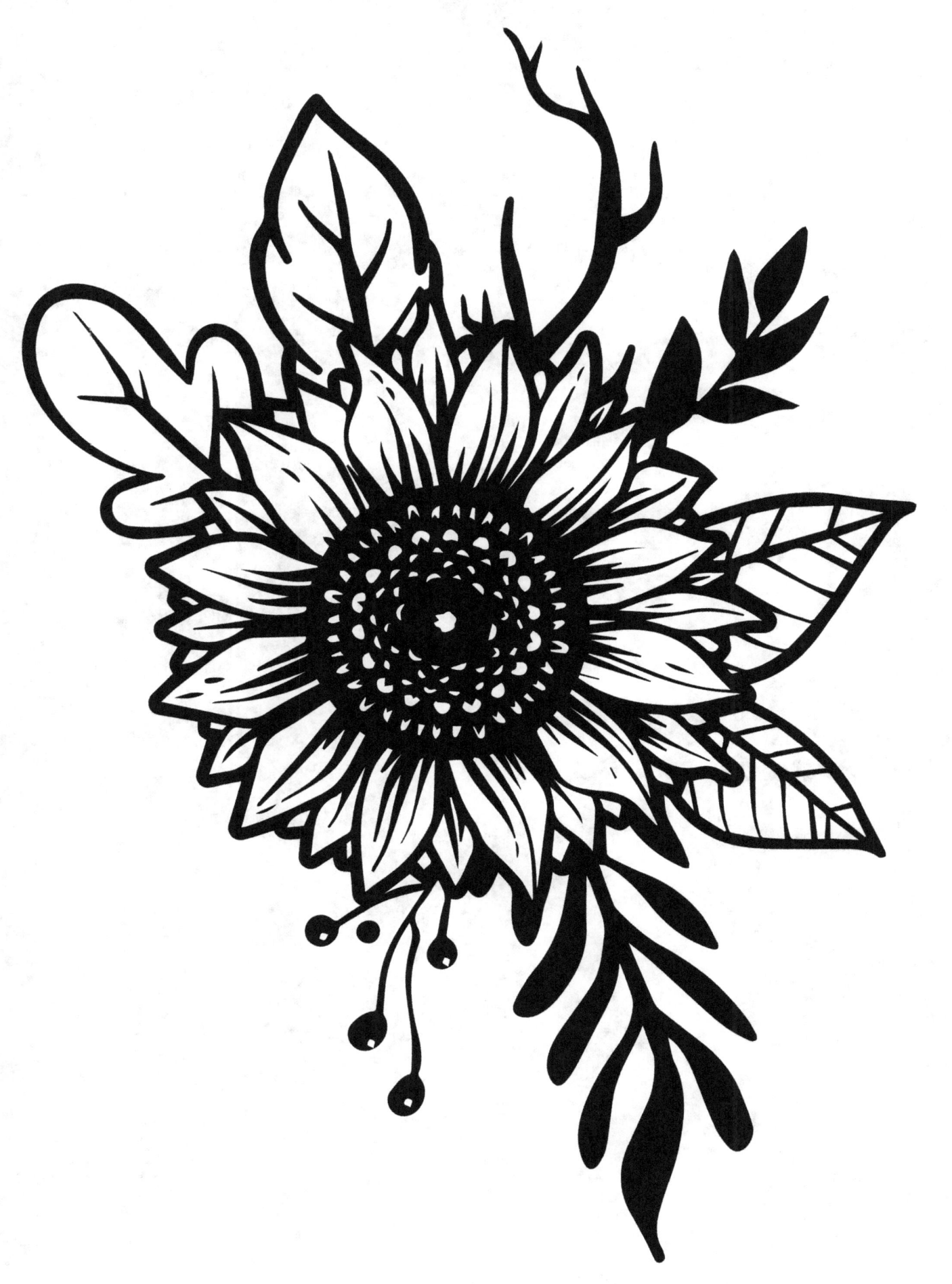

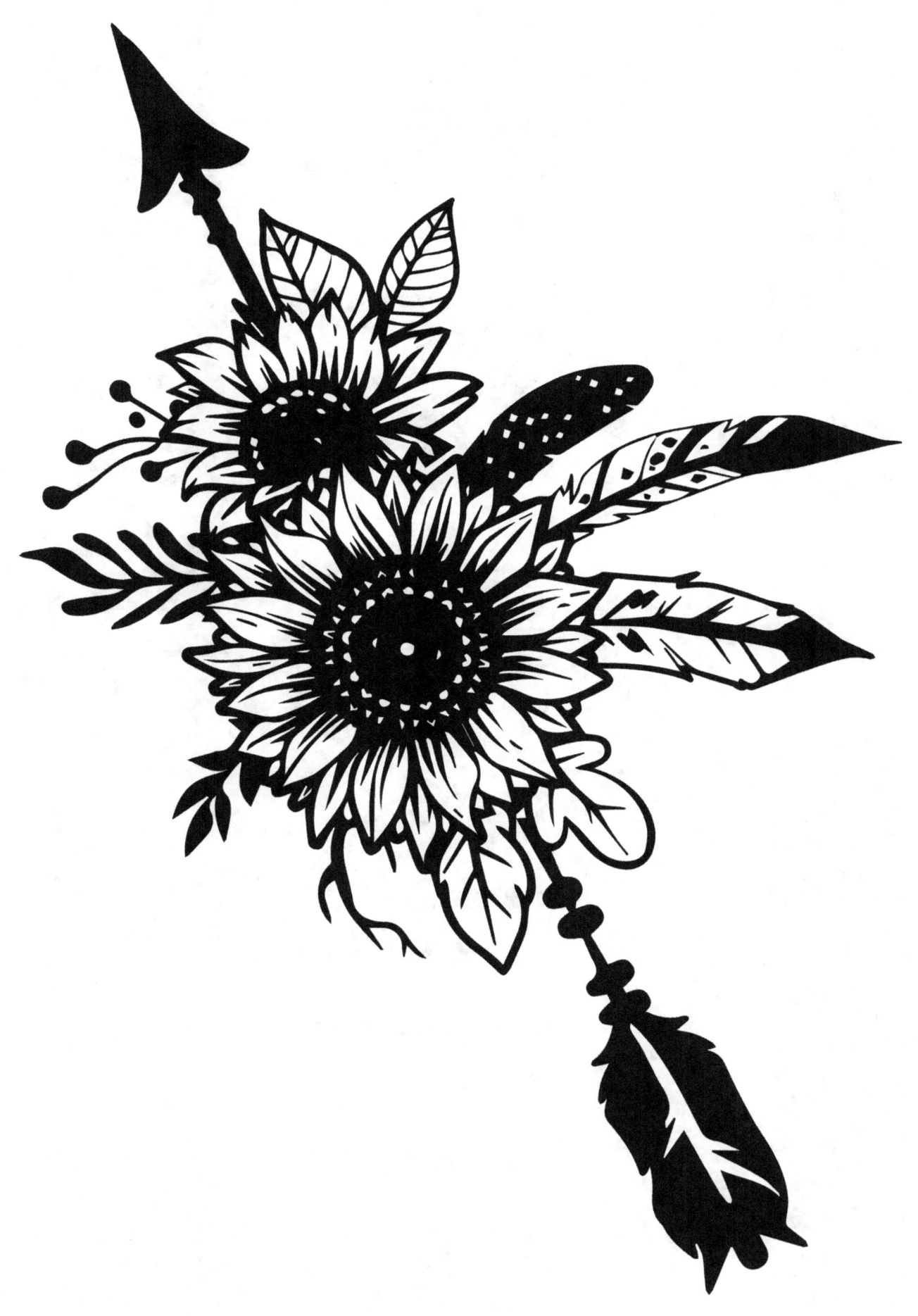

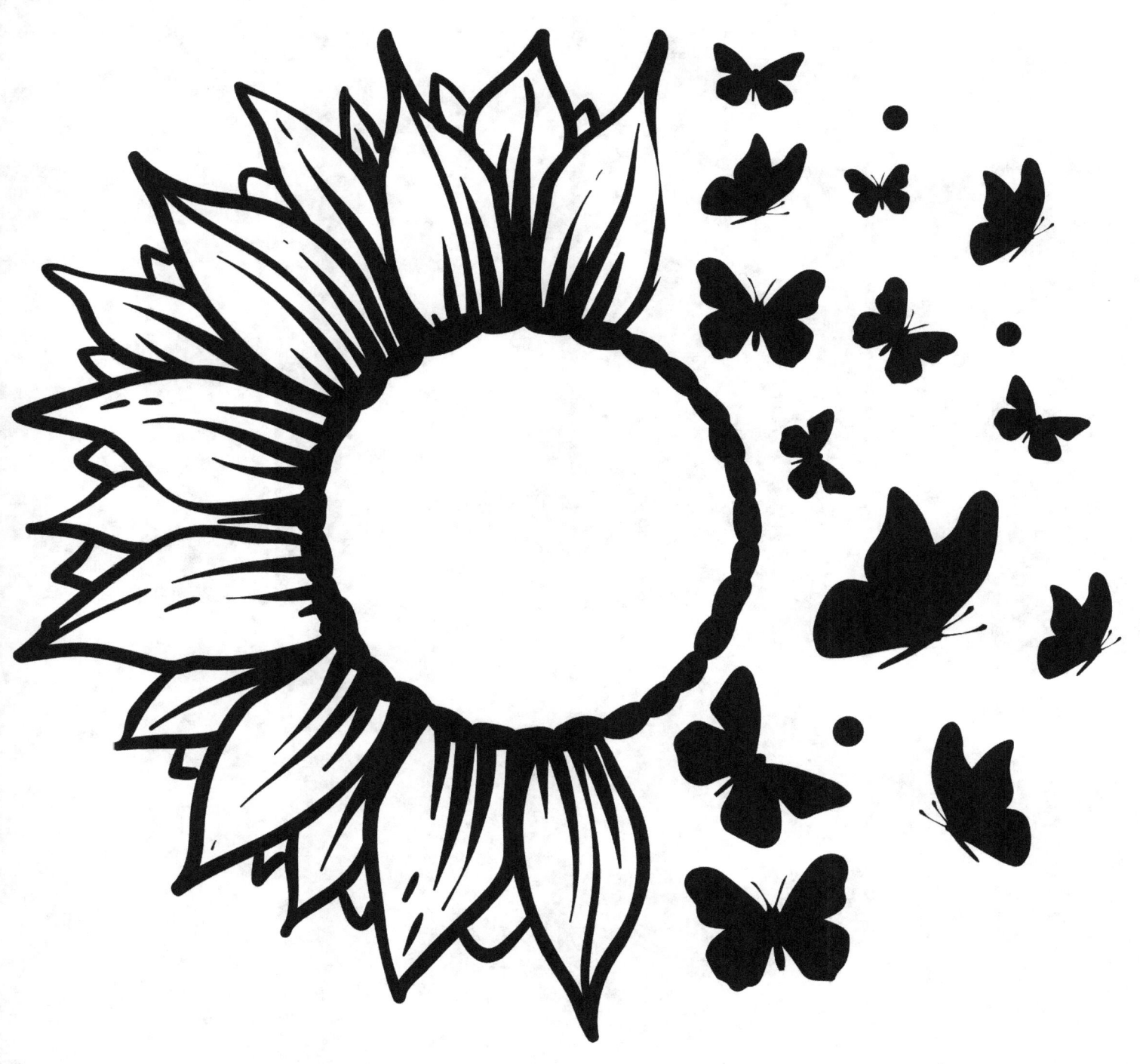

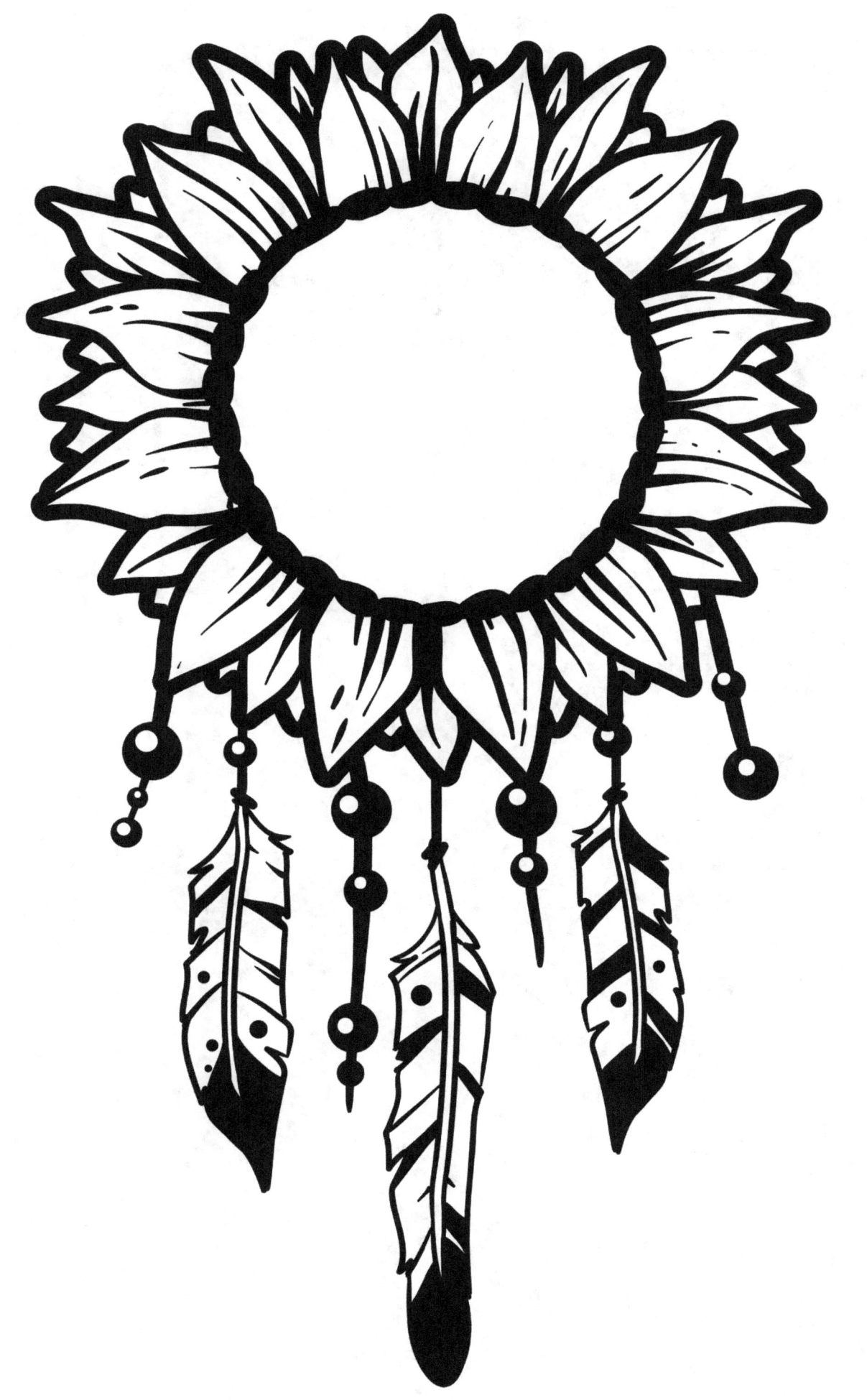

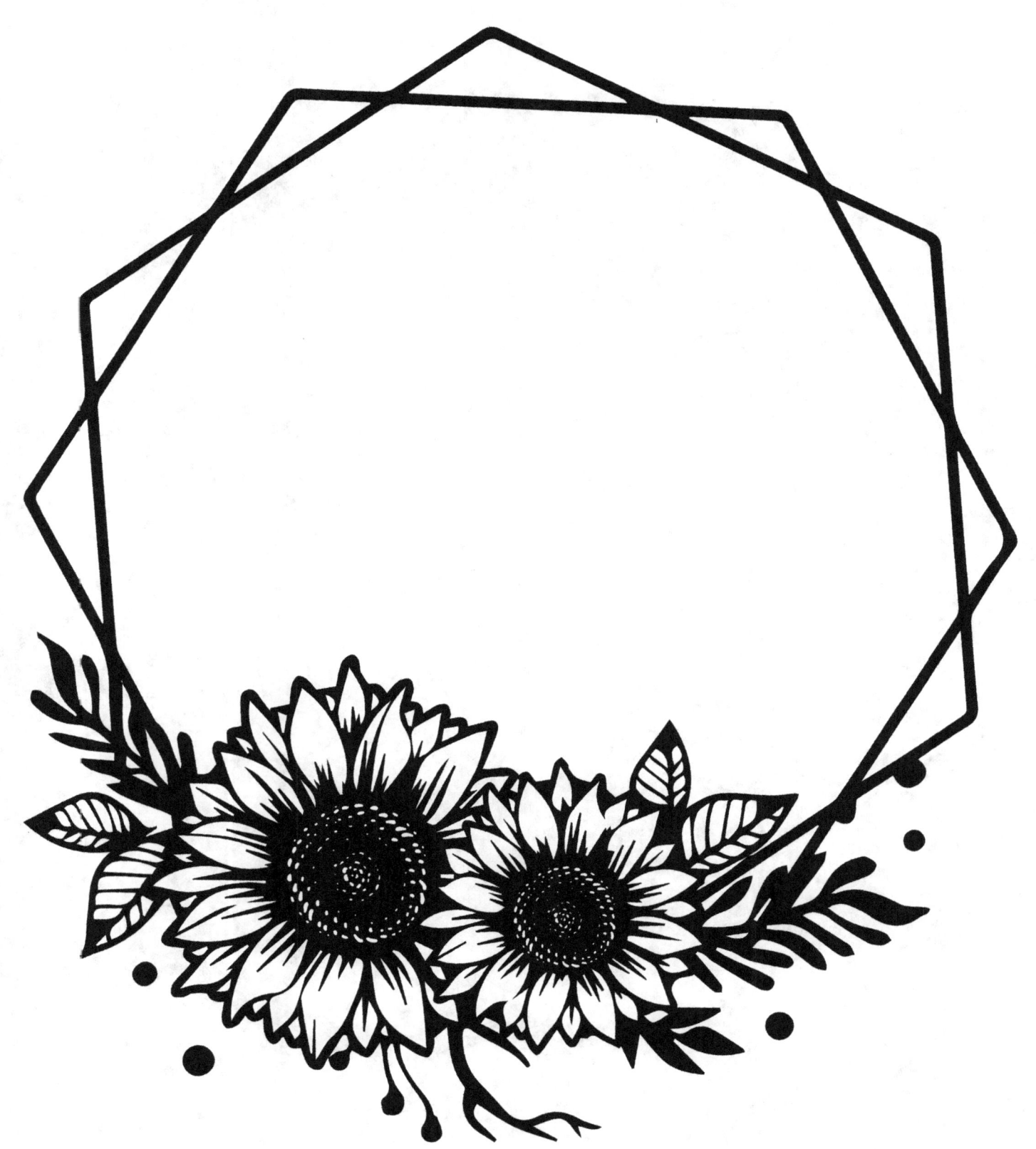

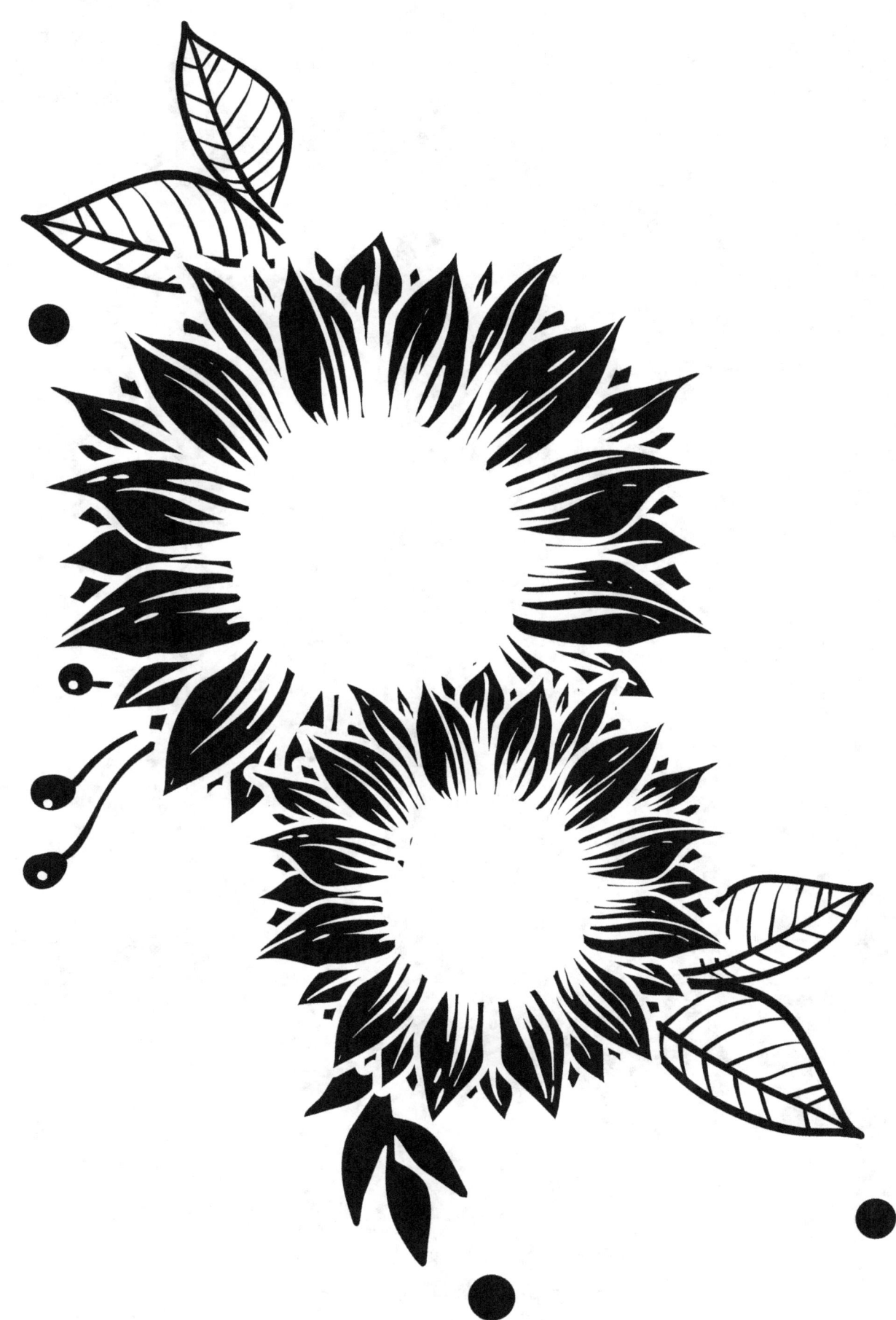

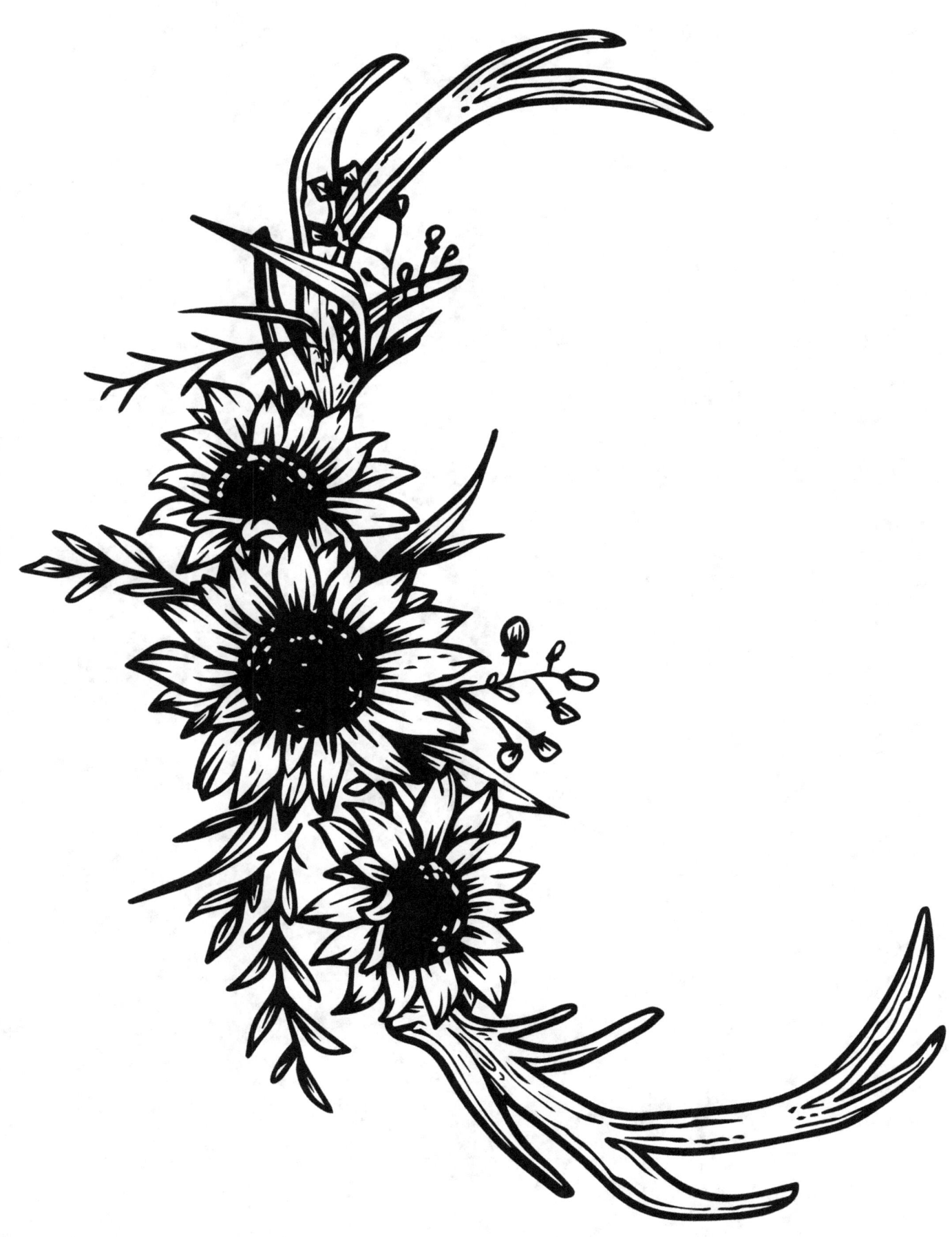

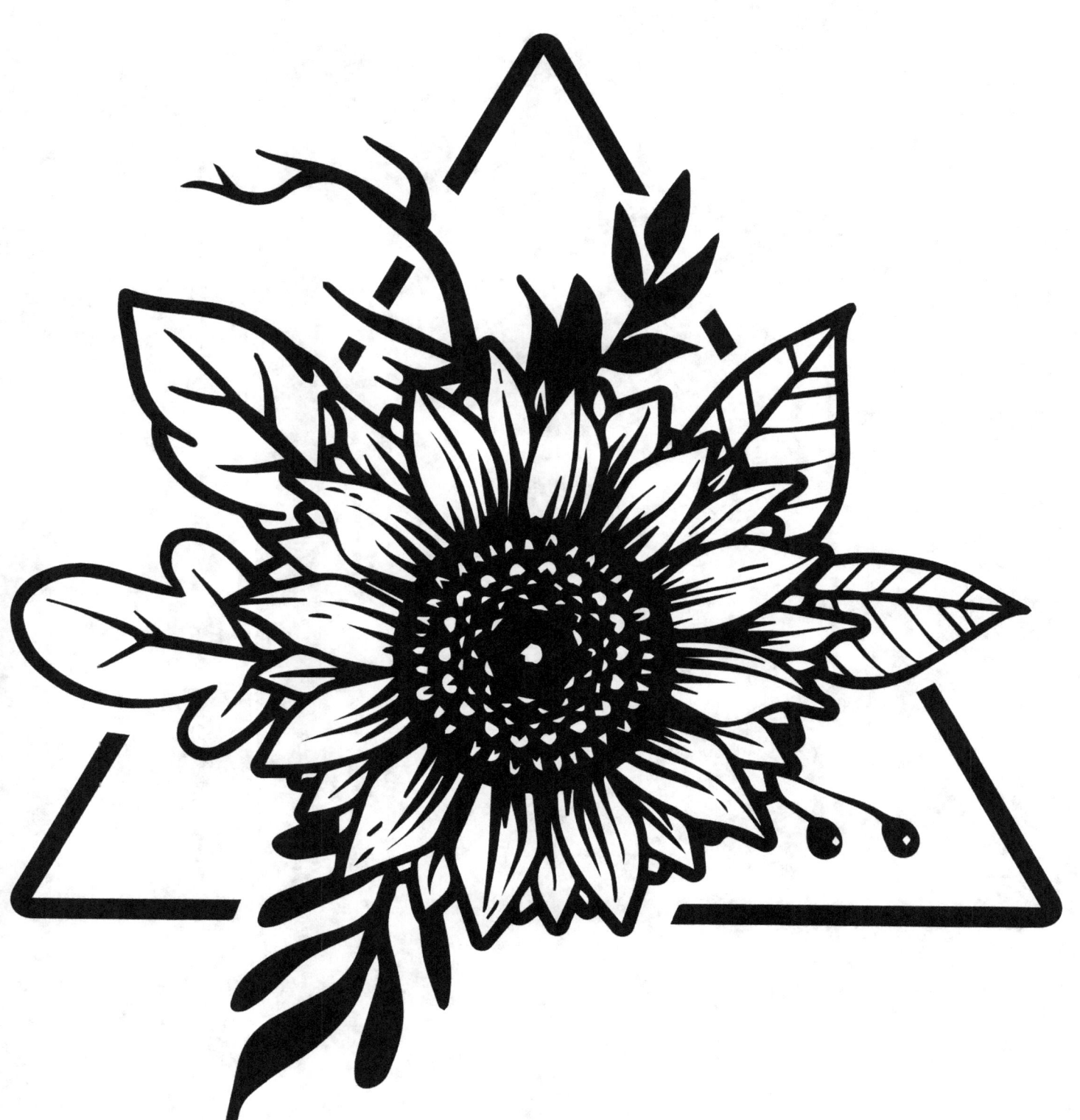

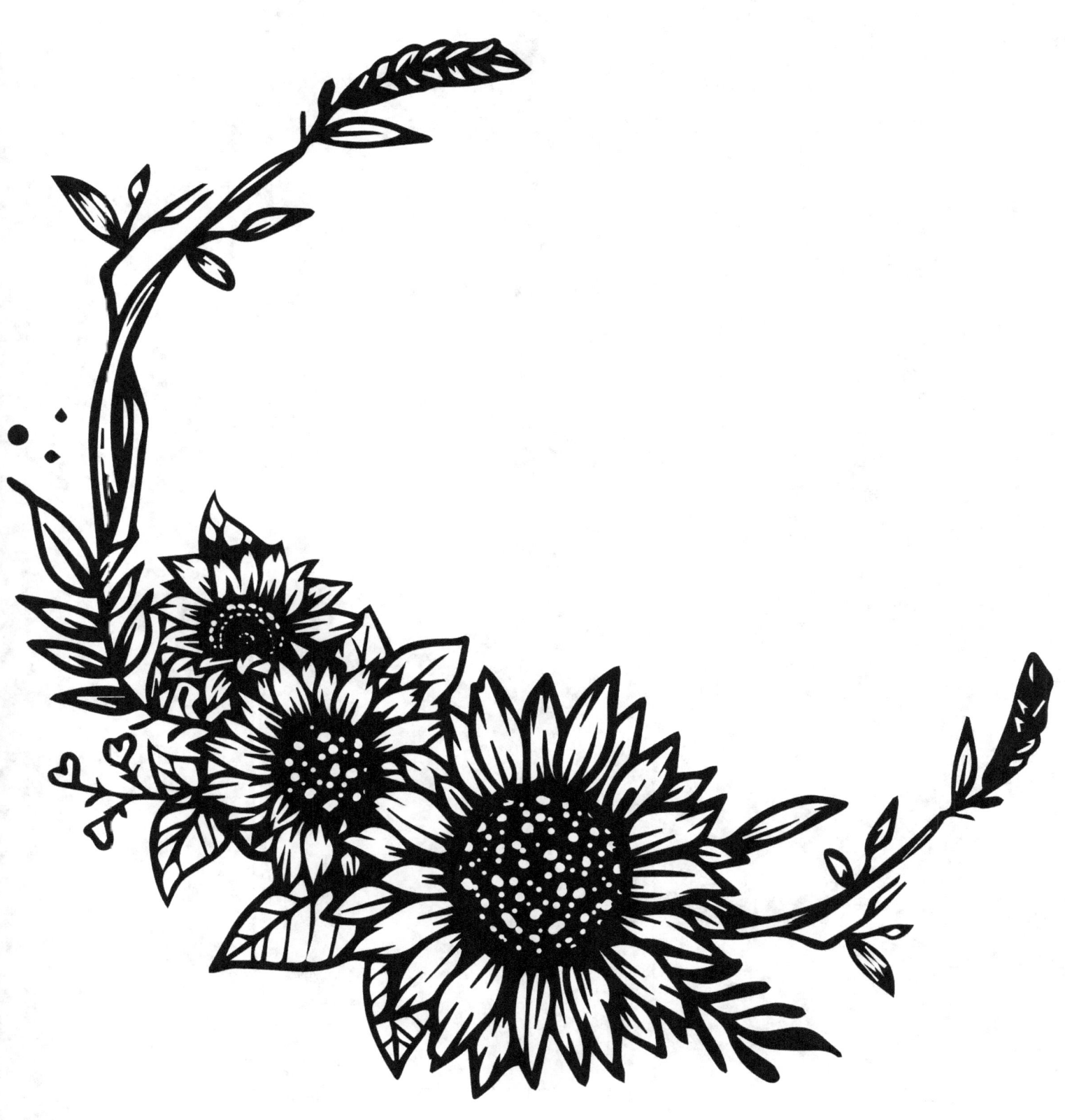

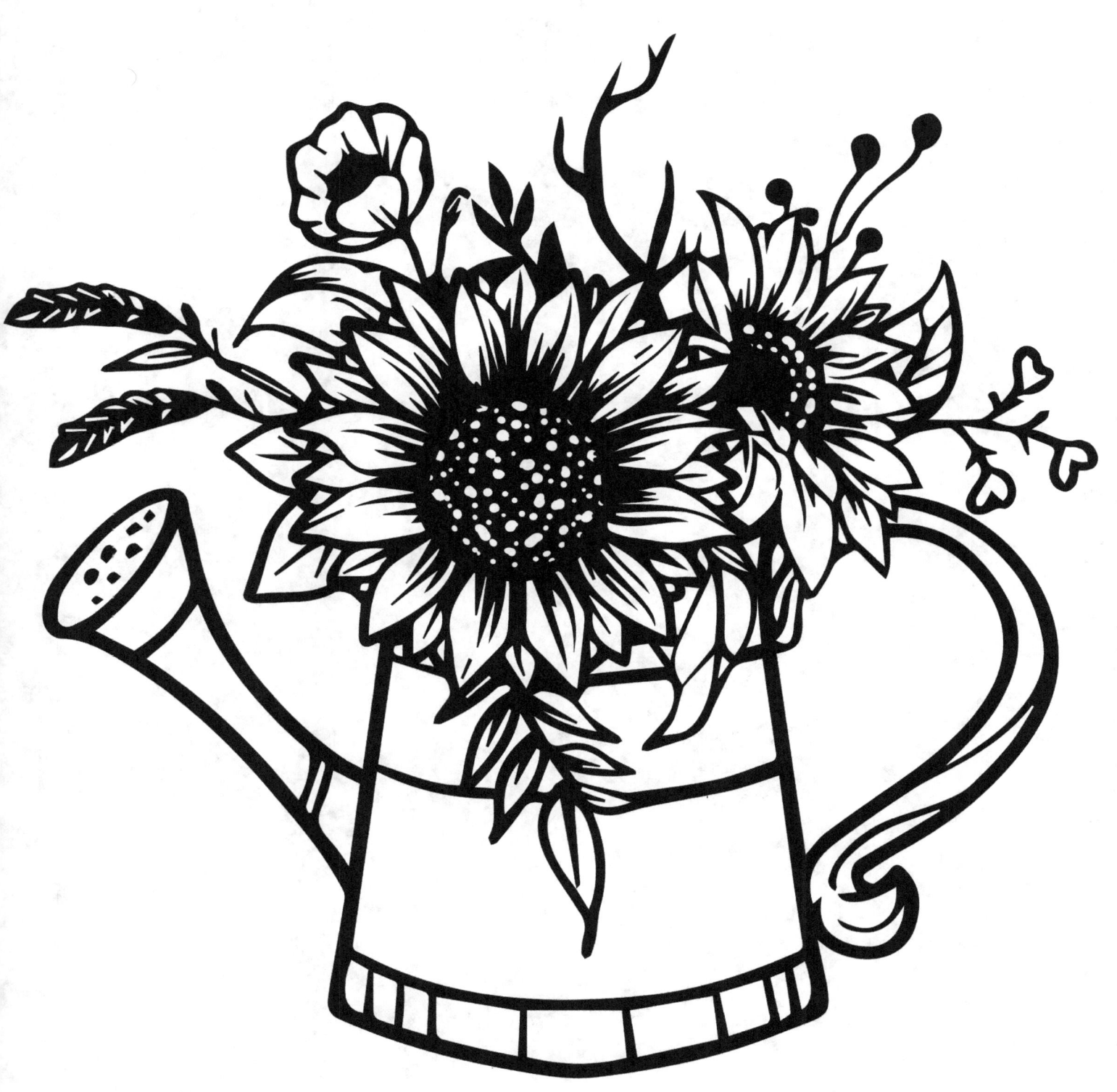

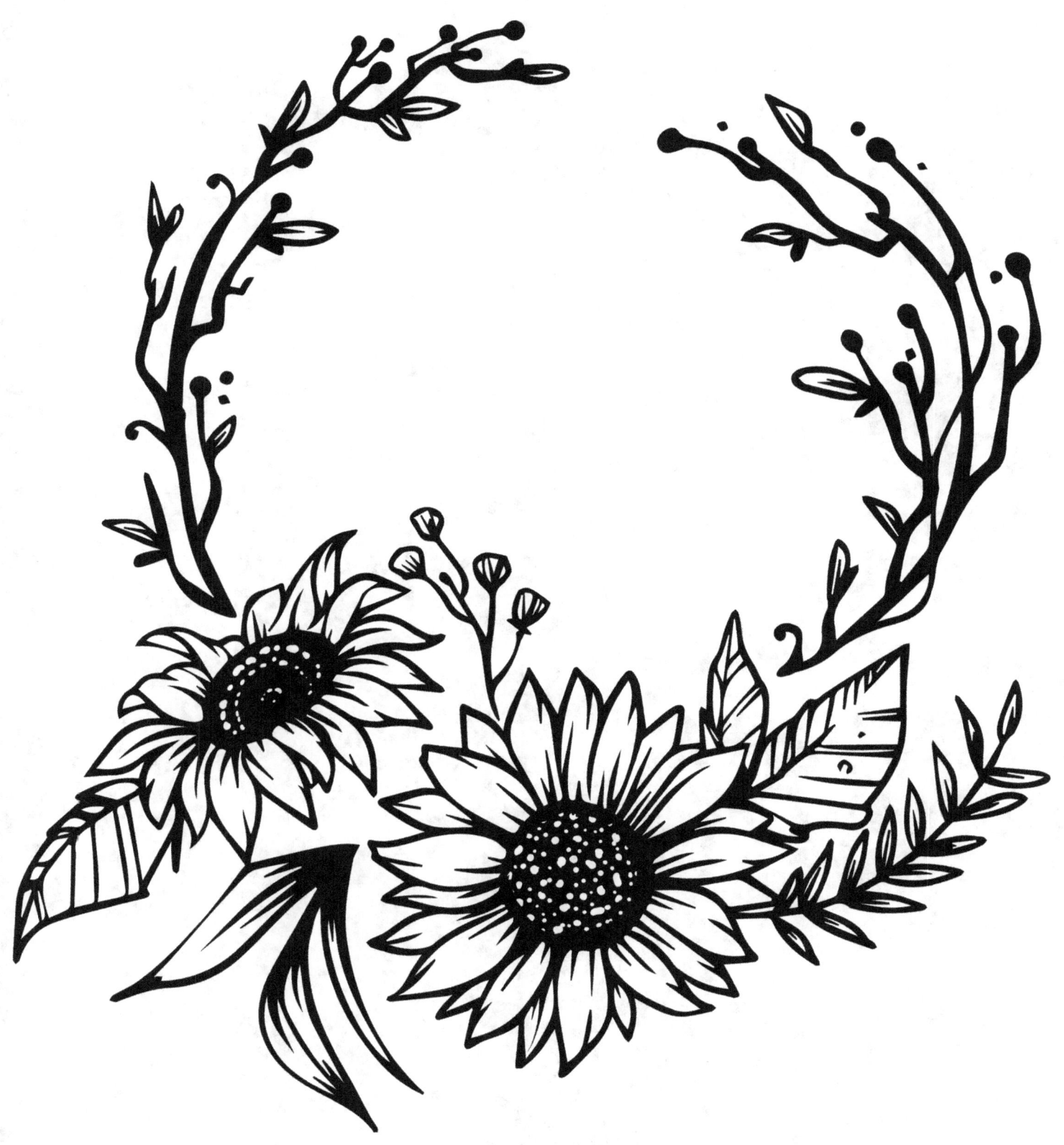

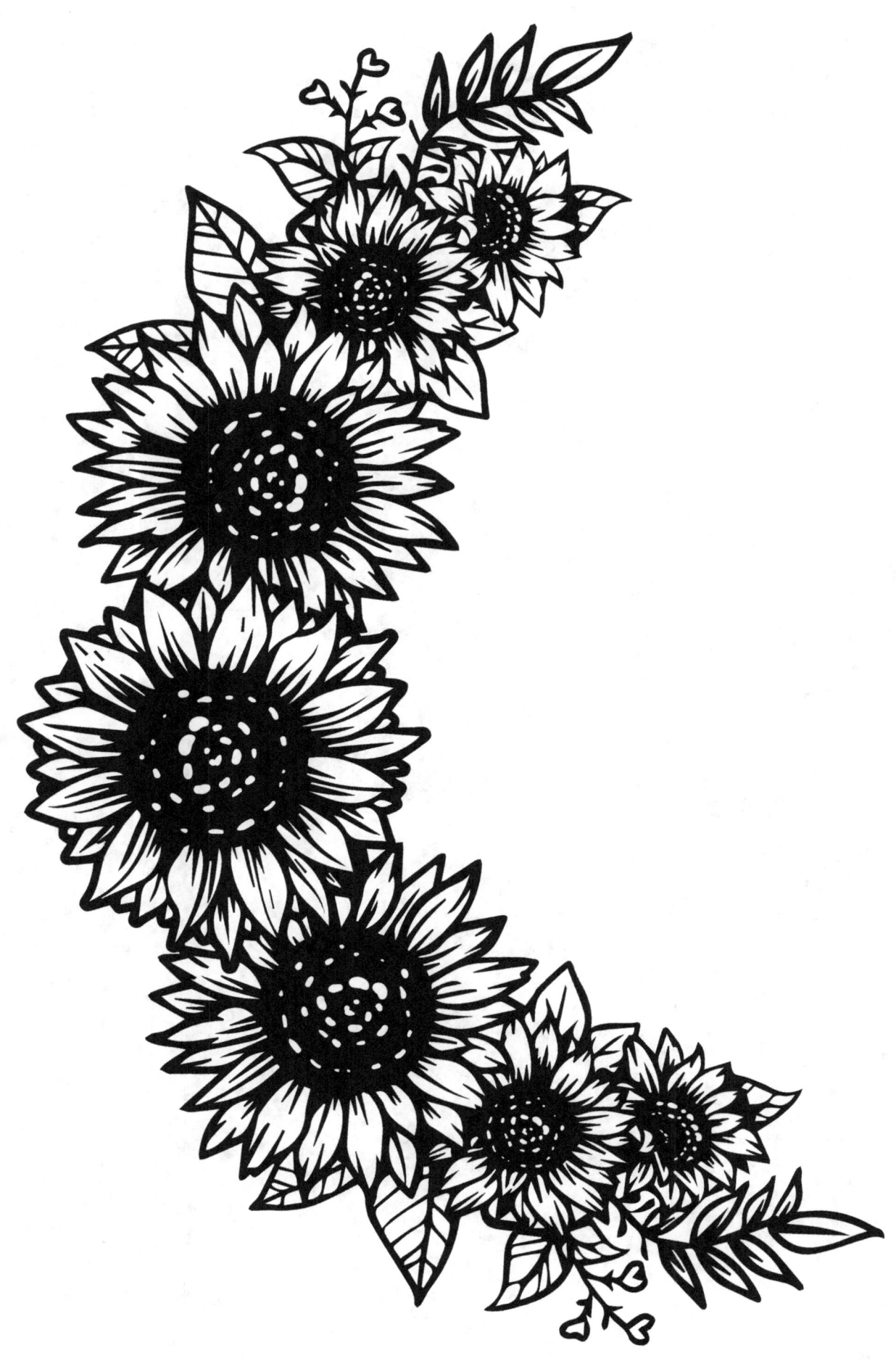

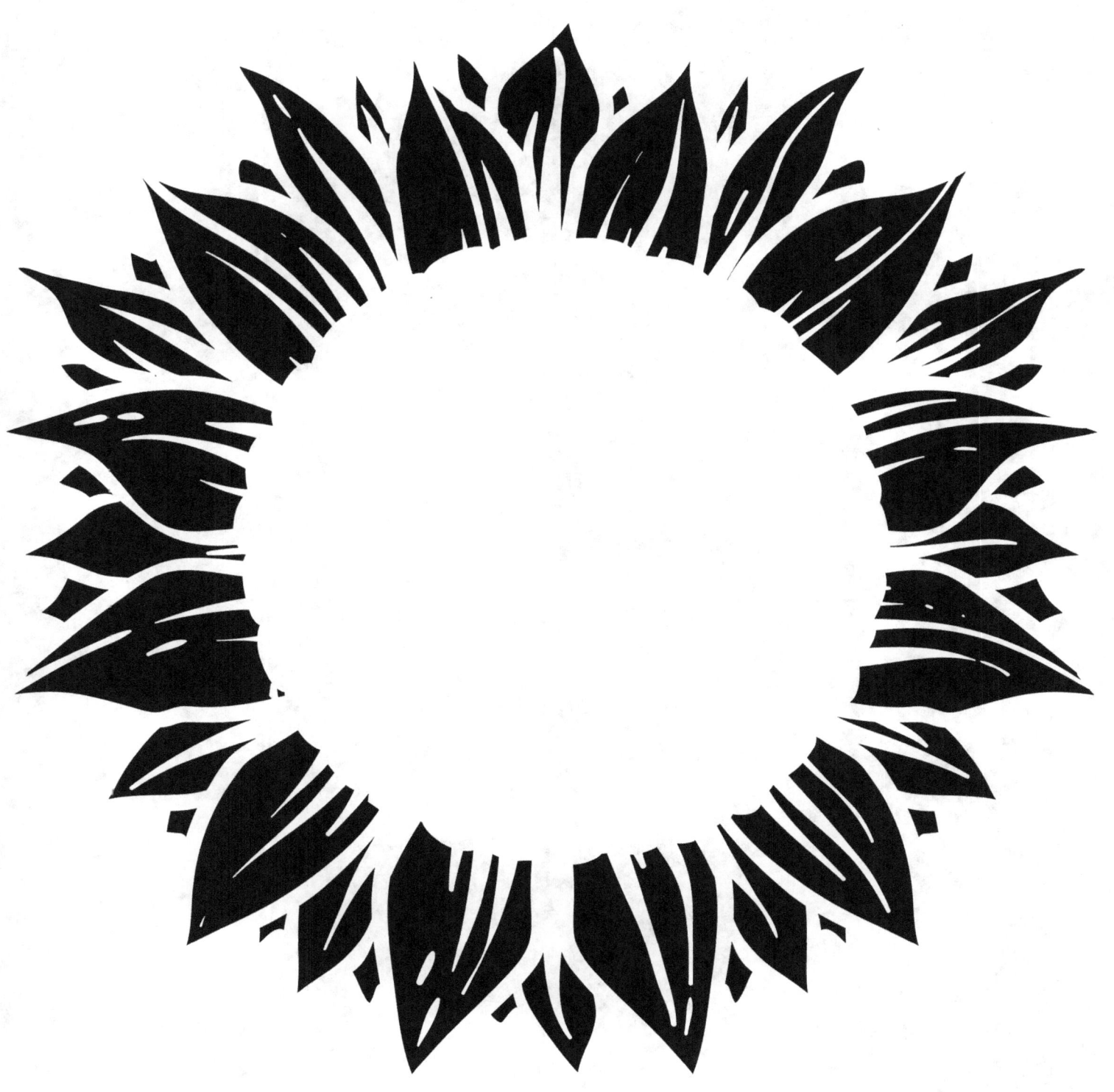

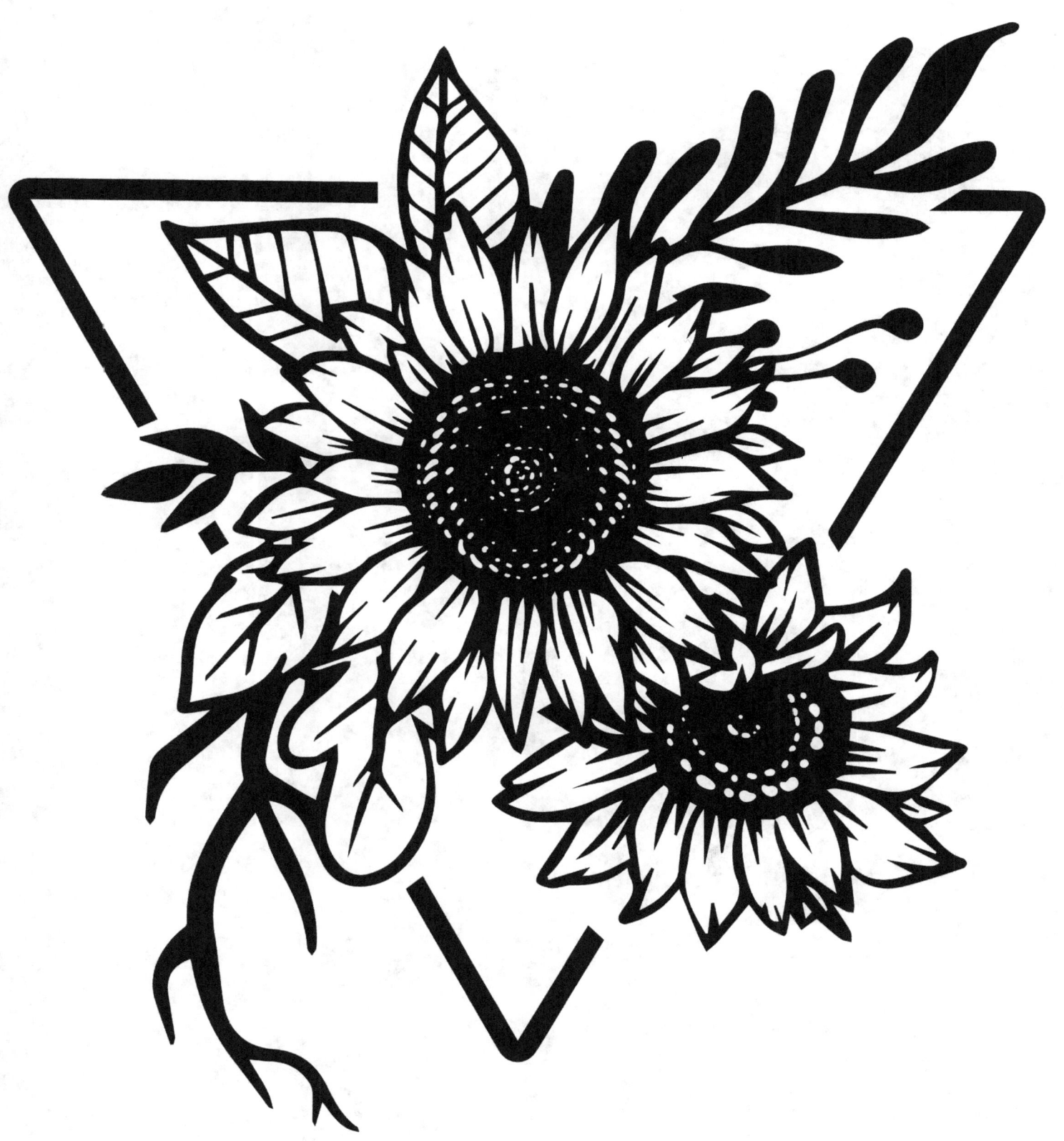

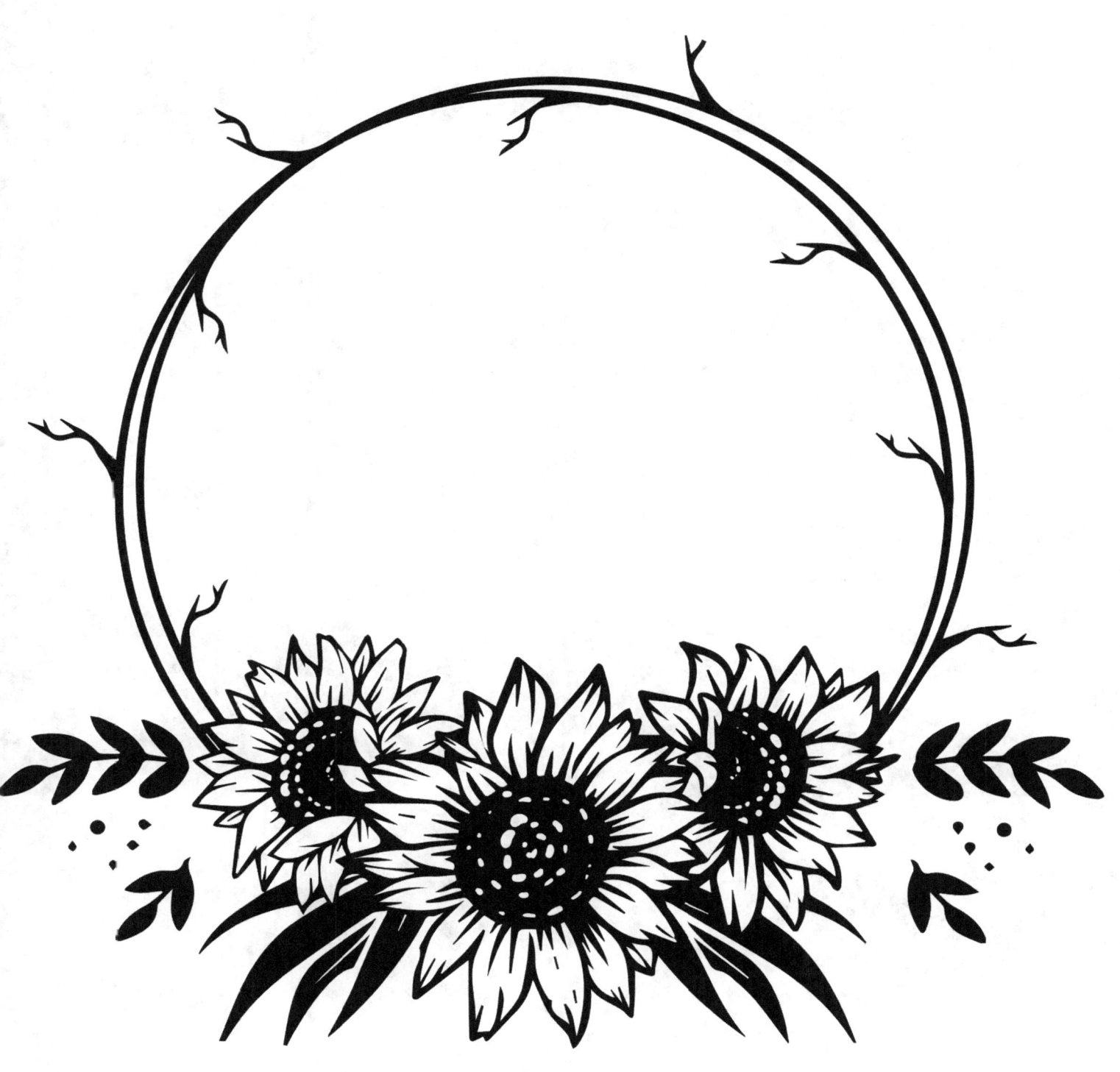

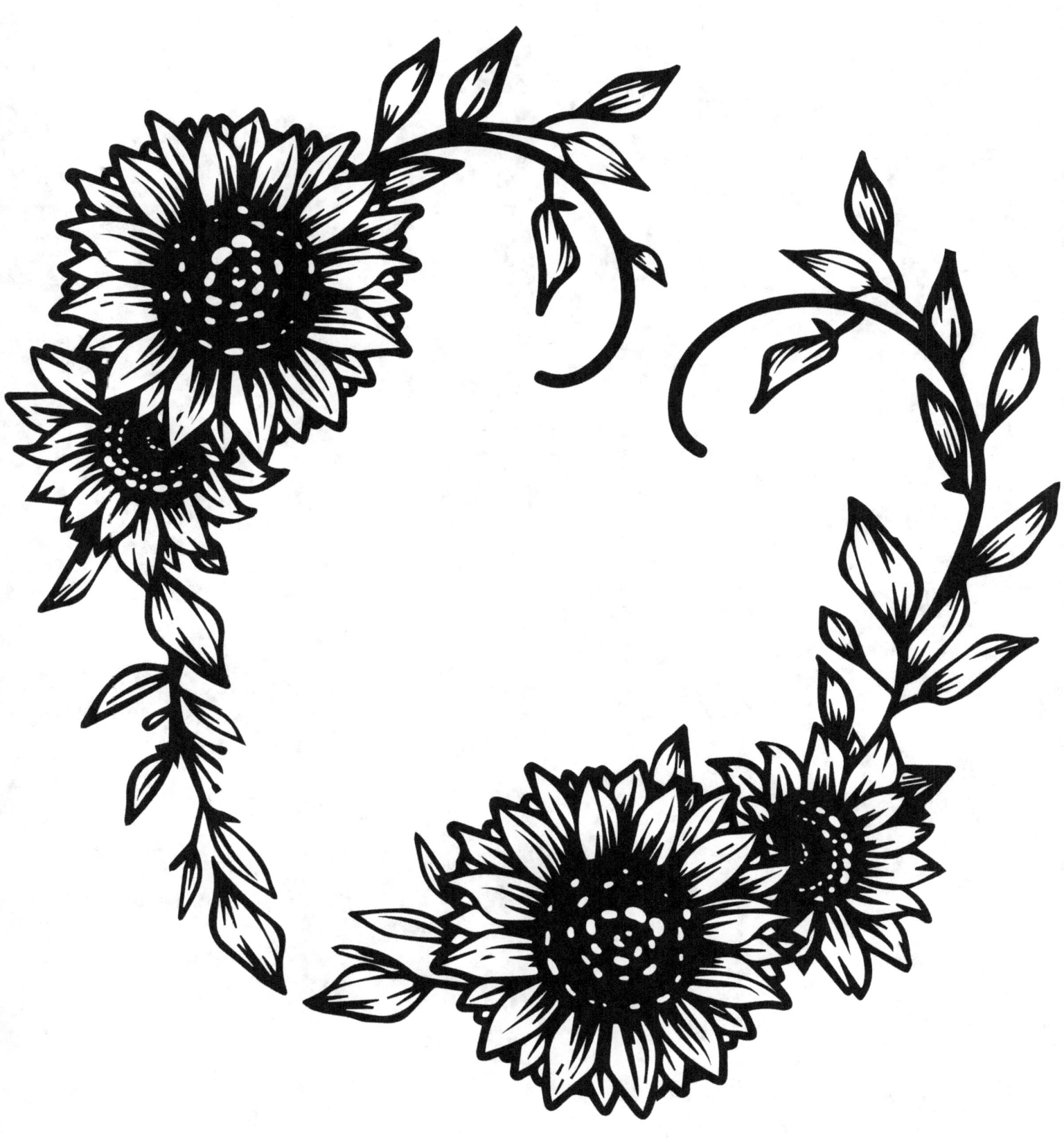

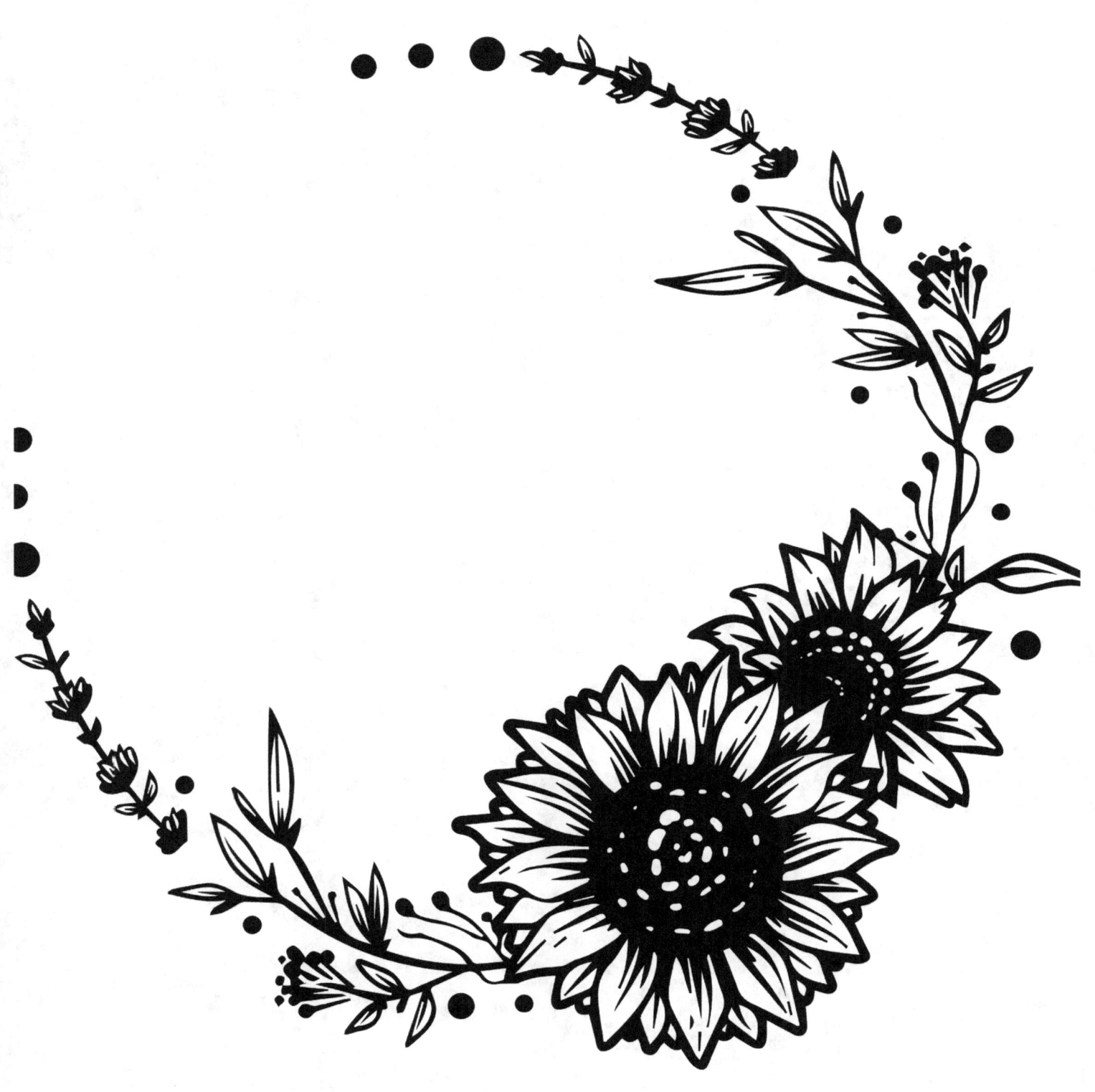

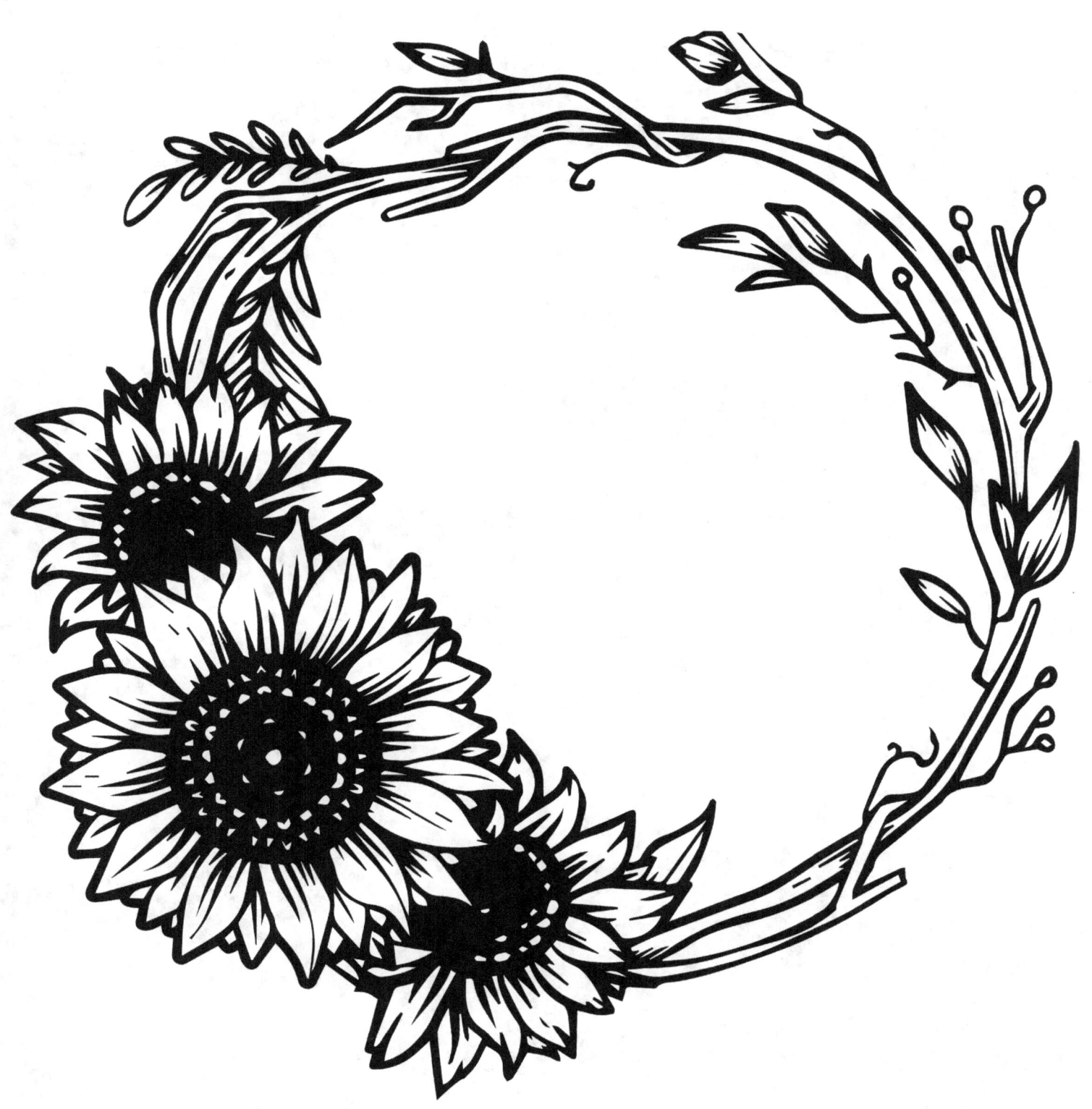

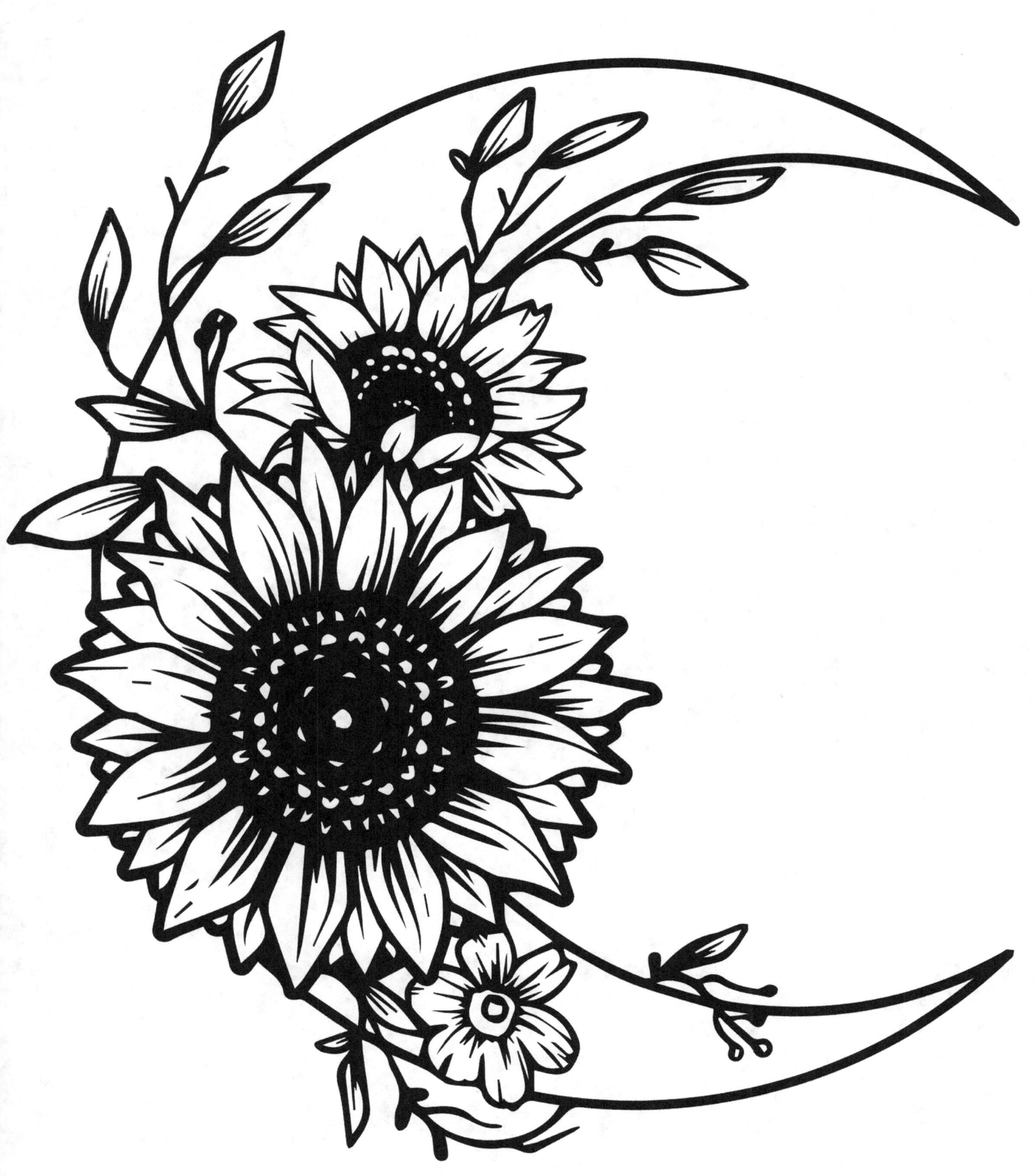

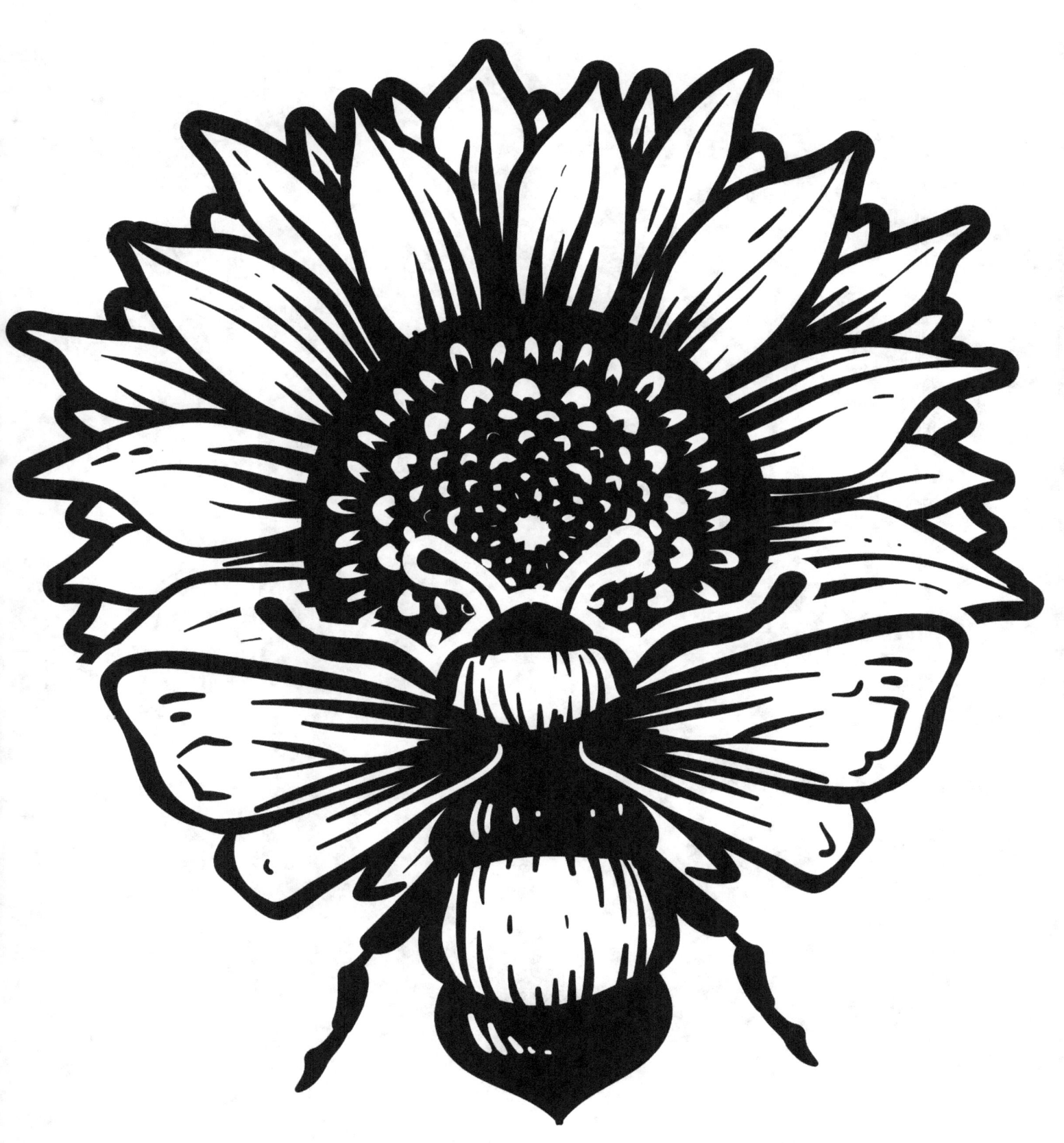

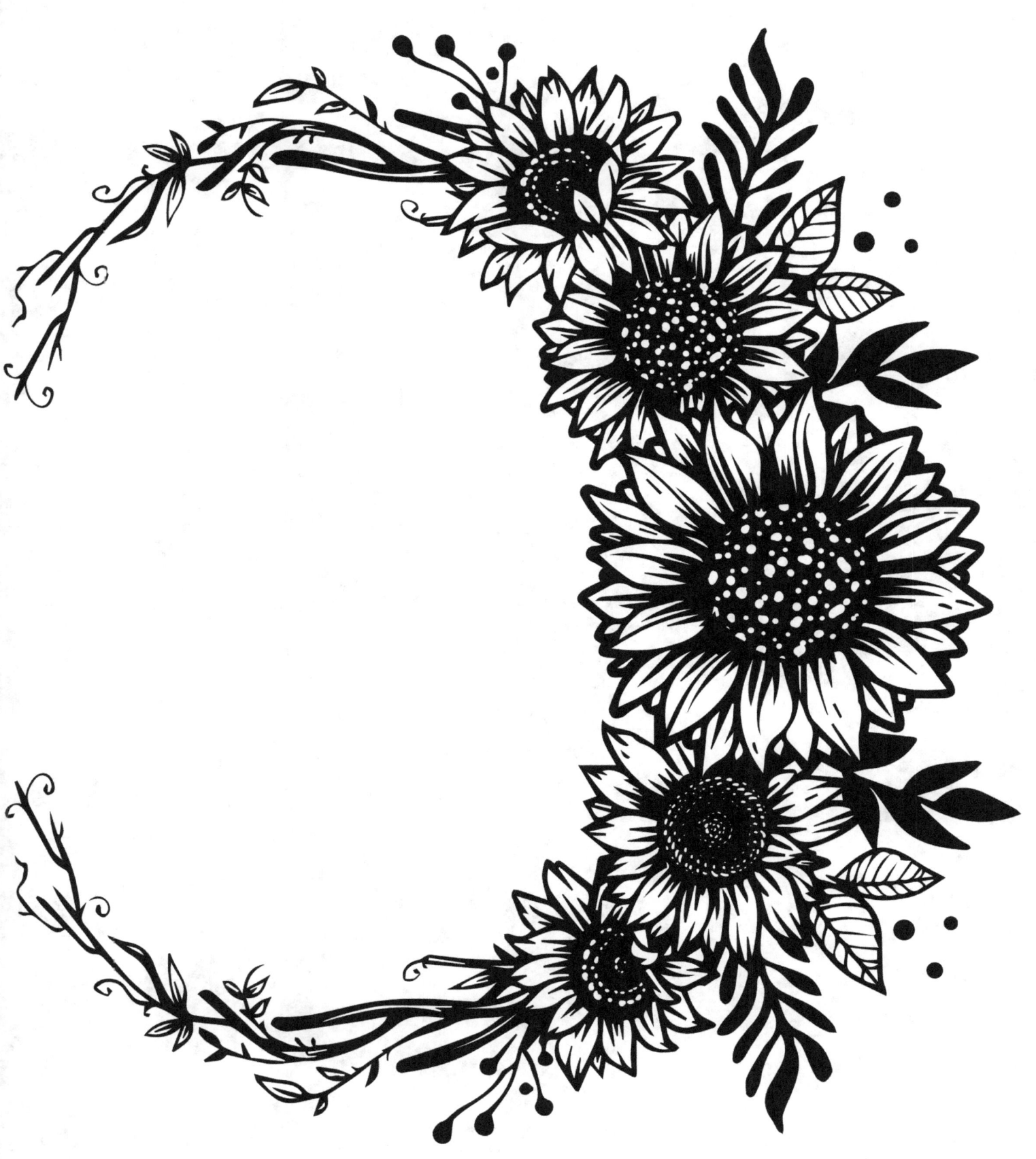

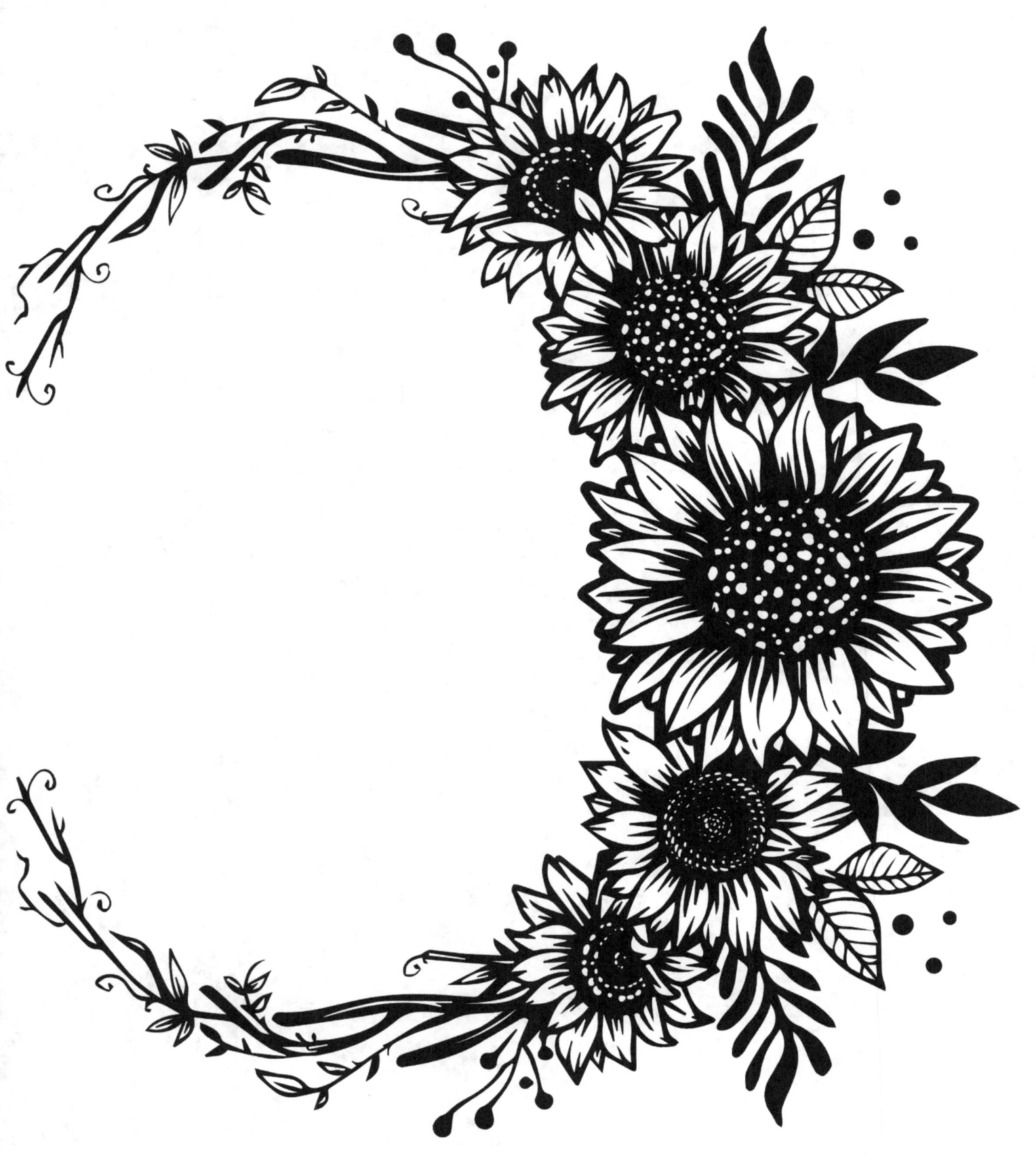

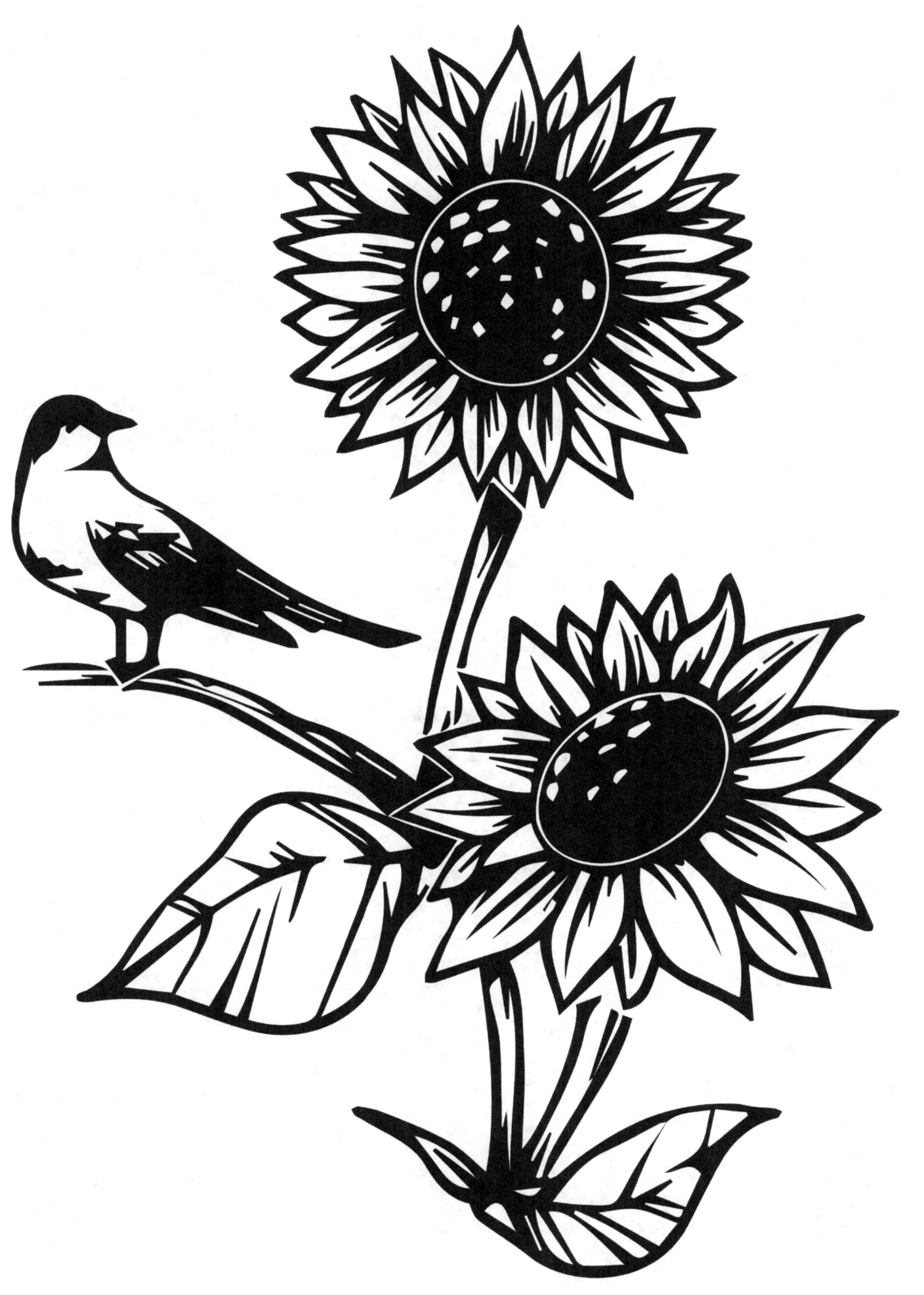

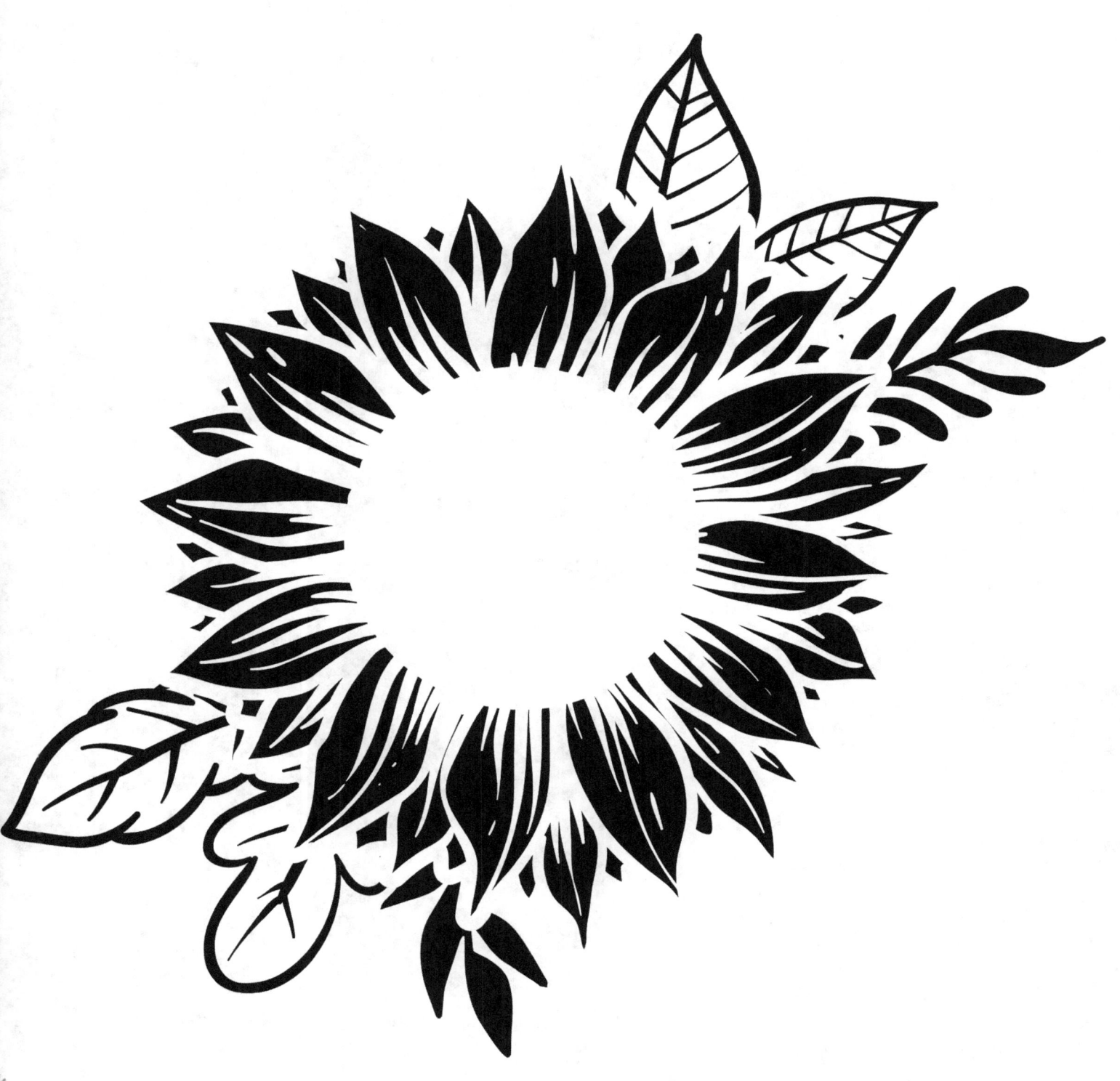

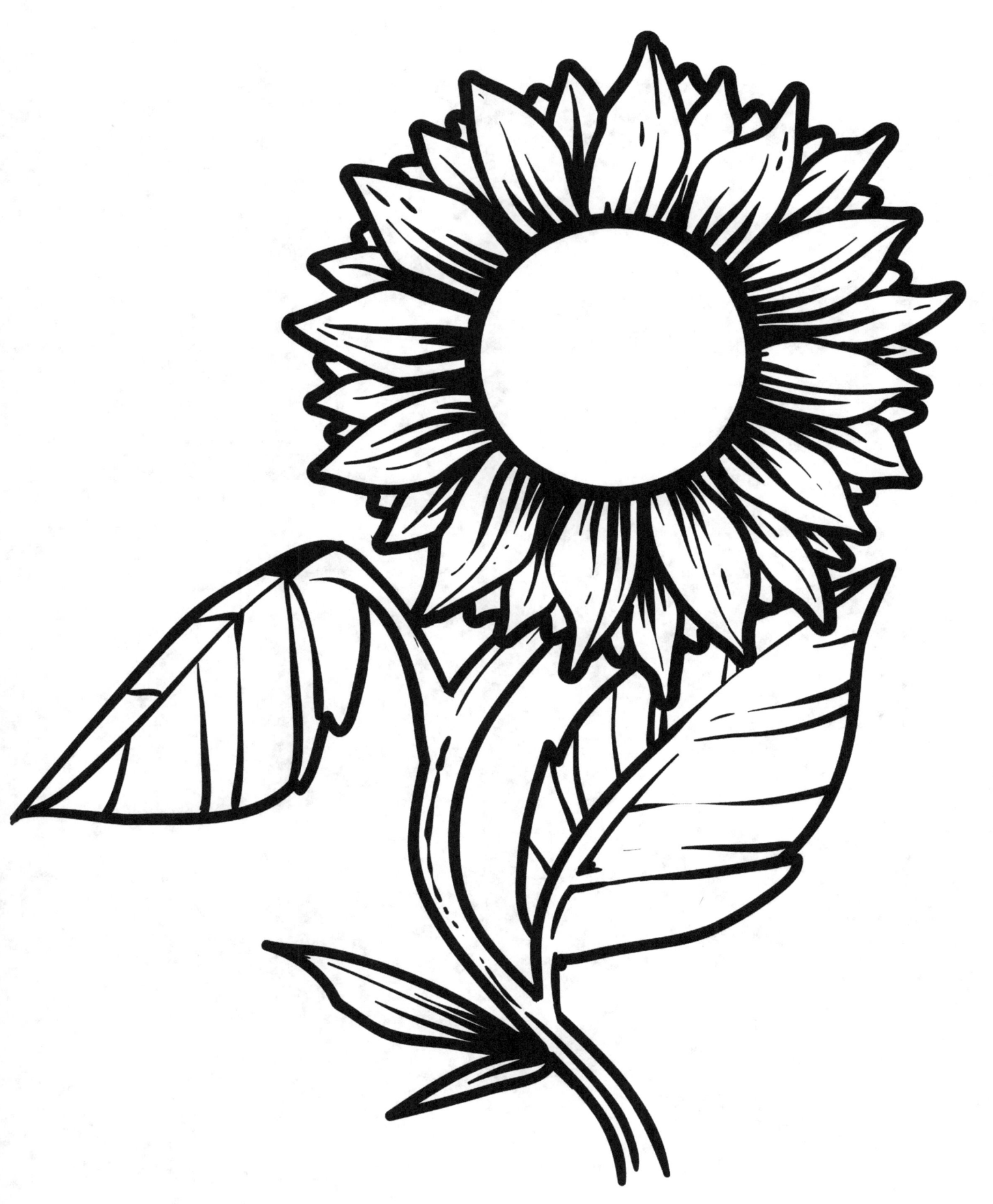

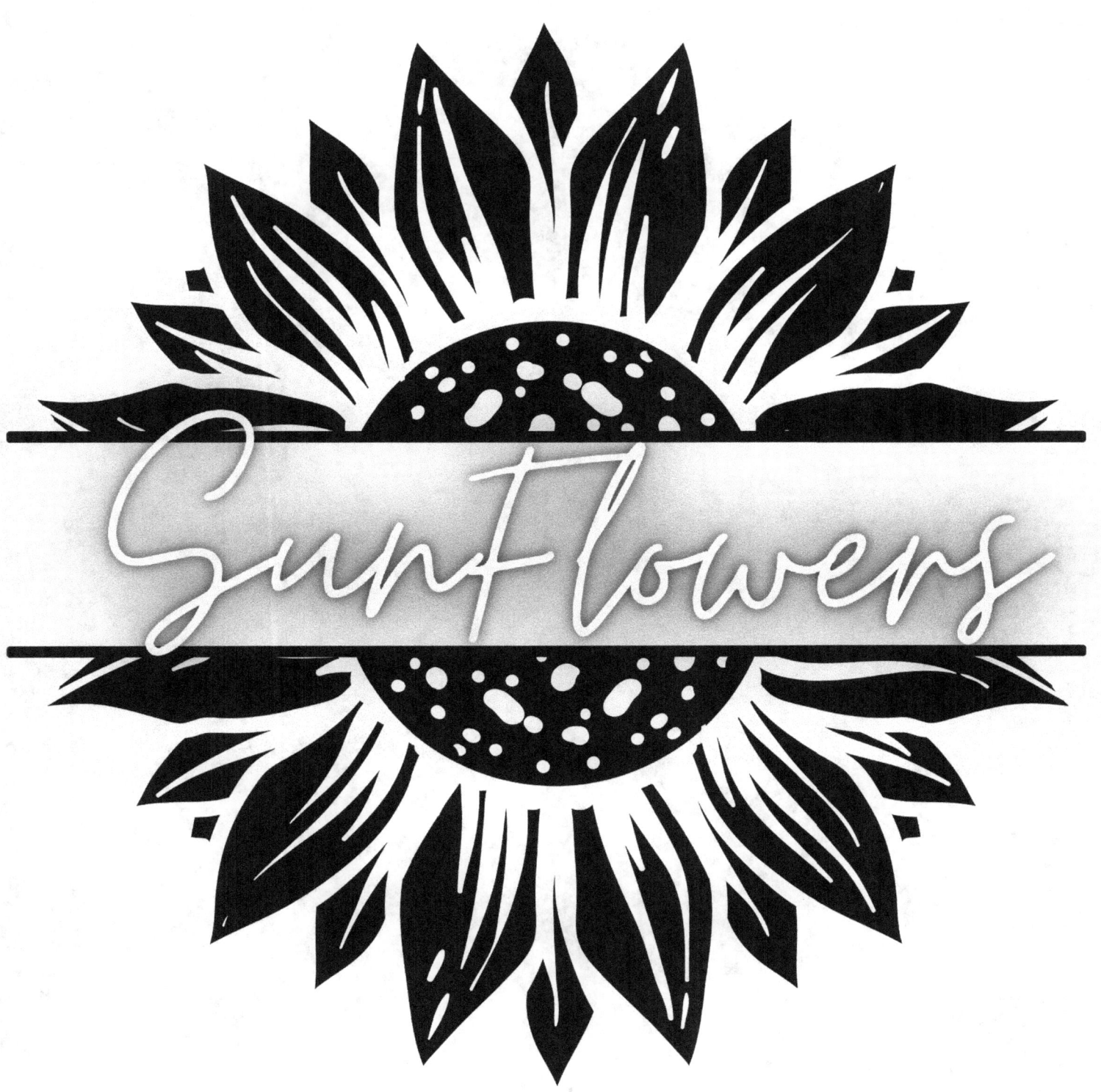

Some of Our Collection

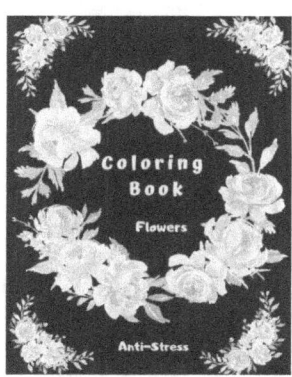
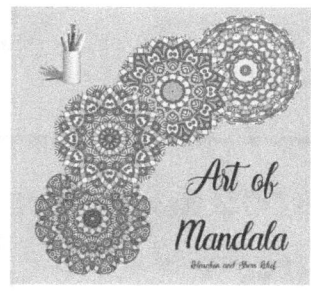
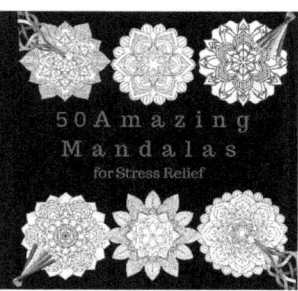
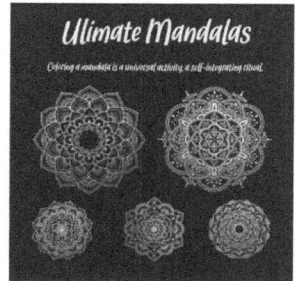
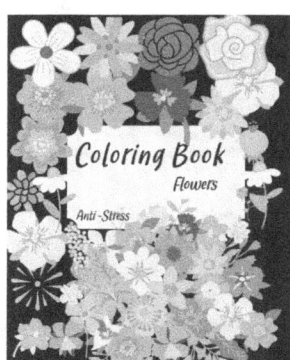
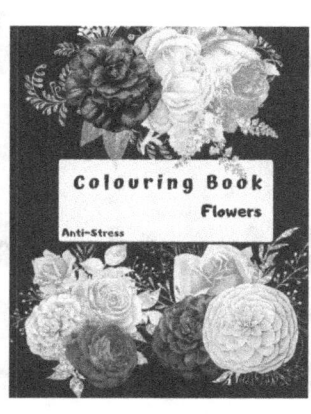
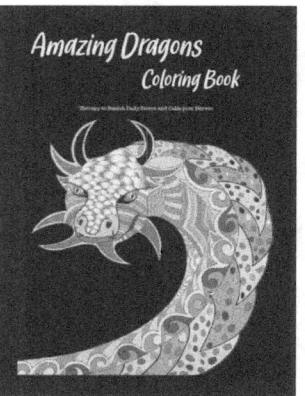
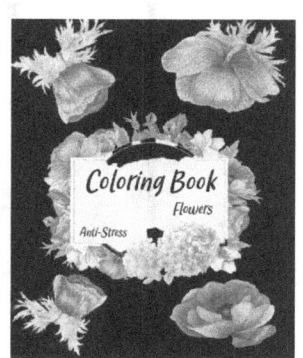
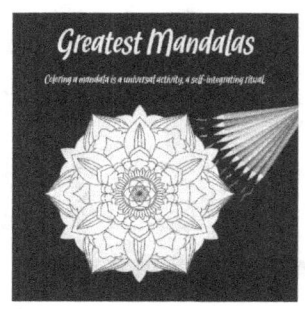
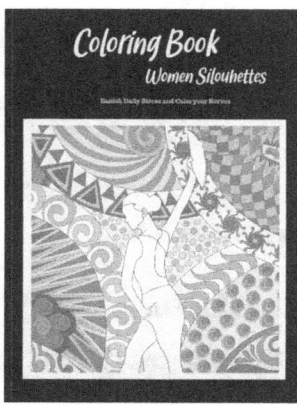
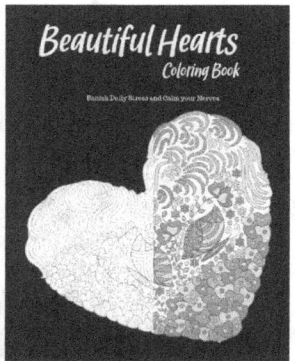
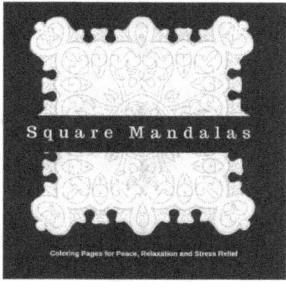

If you can't find the Book that suits you, please let us know at
soumapublisher@gmail.com

We'll be happy to create it and make it available on Amazon You will receive
a free e-copy as a thank you.

This Book is dedicated to Coloring Book Lovers

If You Enjoy it , Please consider Leaving a review

For any suggestions, please send us message to : soumapublisher@gmail.com

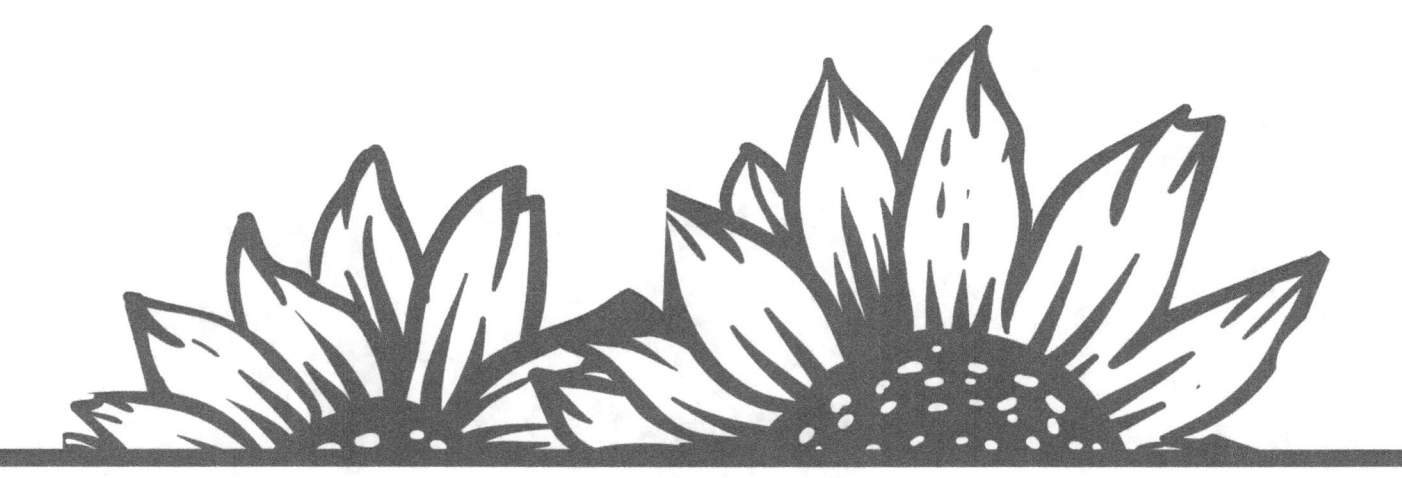

Thank You!

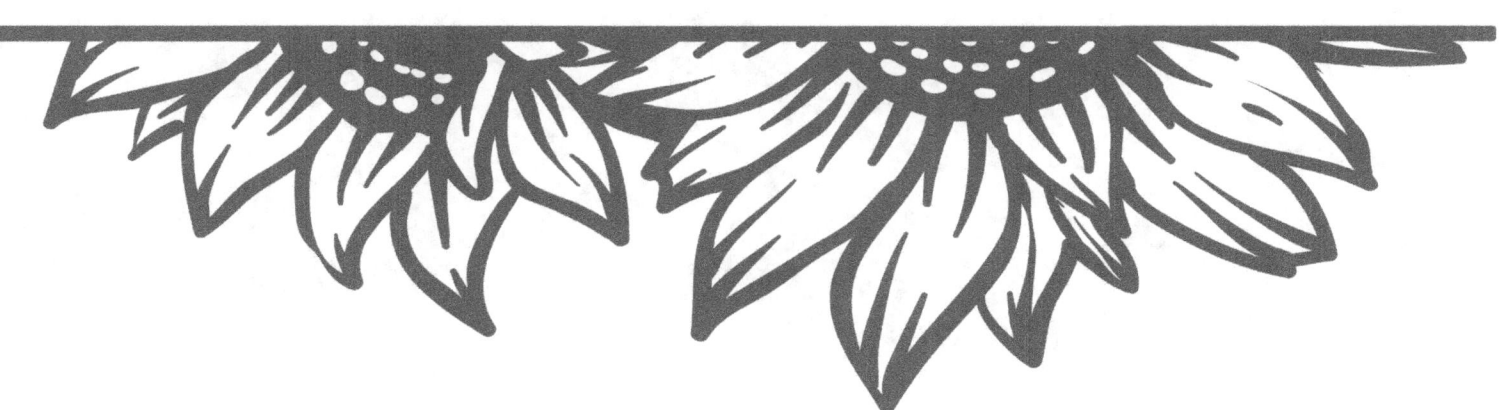

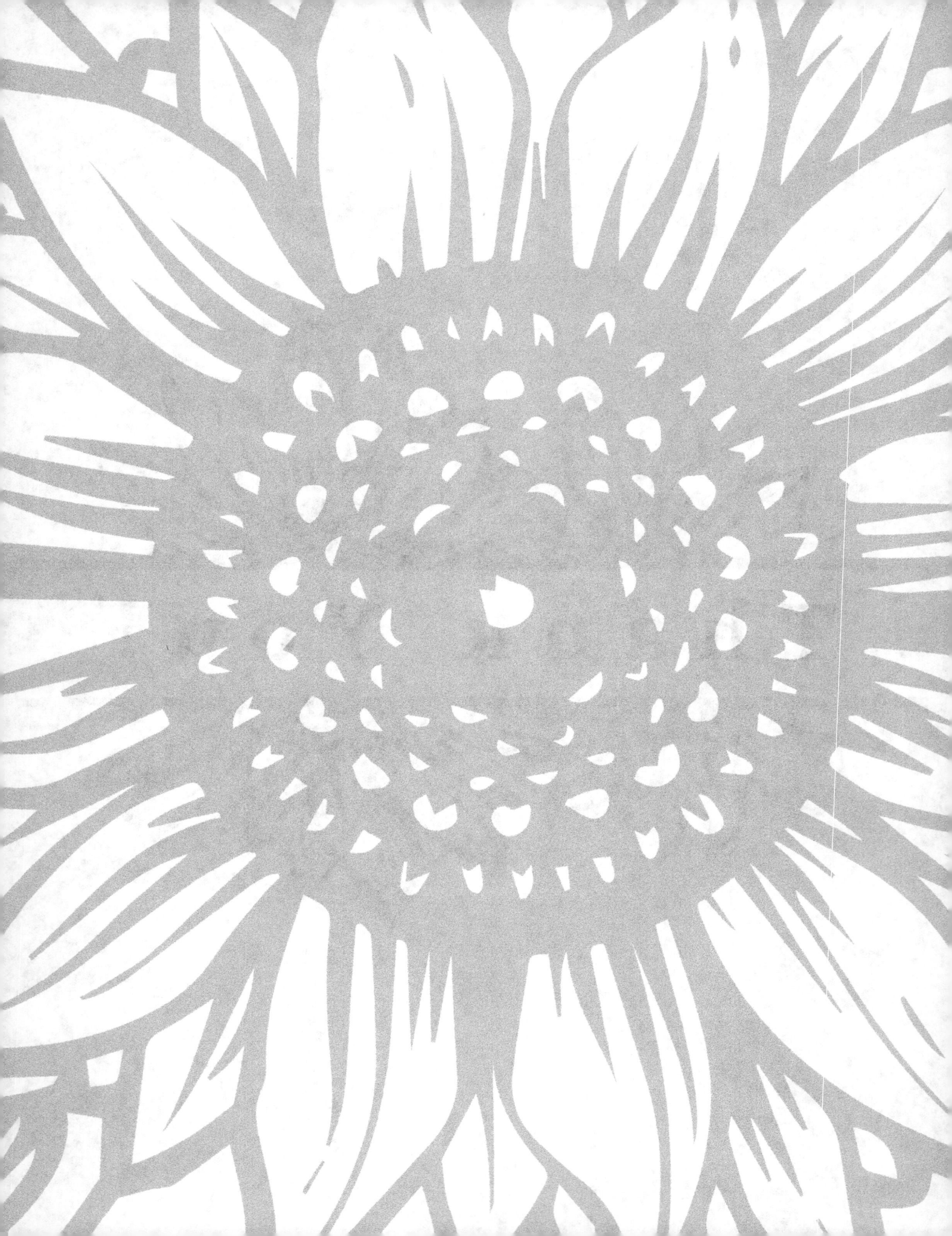

www.ingramcontent.com/pod-product-compliance
Lightning Source LLC
Chambersburg PA
CBHW081523220526
45467CB00010B/3018